Folk in Cornwall
Music and musicians of the 60's revival

Rupert White

Front cover: Wizz Jones on Great Western Beach, Newquay. Back cover Jug band at The Folk Cottage.

ISBN 978-0-9932164-0-4

First published in 2013 by Antenna Publications

Since those summers in Cornwall I have been lucky enough to play all over the world and wherever I go I am sure to meet someone who introduces themselves by saying 'You'll never guess where I first saw you playing'. I pretend to be surprised but I know what they are going to say – The Folk Cottage in Mitchell and we grin at the memory of some wonderful, crazy, happy times.

Ralph McTell

This book is based on interviews and correspondence with Clive Palmer,
Martin Val Baker, John 'The Fish' and Carrie Langford, Gypsy Dave Mills,
Wizz Jones, Ralph McTell, Des Hannigan, John and Jane Sleep, Judi Rea, Sue
Ellery, Rosemary Tawney, Richard and Jan Gendall, Jill Johnson, Mike Sagar,
John Bidwell, Mick Bennett, Toni Carver, Pete Berryman, Alan Tunbridge,
Jonathon Coudrille, Jane Val Baker, Susie and Ken Smith, Michael Chapman,
Mervyn Davey, Donovan, David Dearlove, Mike Silver, Mic McCreadie,
Chrissy Quayle, Noel Murphy, Ian Anderson, Pete Stanley & Bob Butler.

And the biographies of Donovan, Ralph McTell & Clive Palmer together with
Dick Halliwell's 'Count House to Cottage' radio documentary, PhD thesis
and other articles by Merv Davey, Martin Val Baker's memoirs, Mick
Bennett's Folk Cottage Journals (www.mickbennettcobpsychfolk.com) and the
excellent website www.wizzjones.com.

Fascinating anecdotes and recollections have been shared on Facebook by
many others. (http://www.facebook.com/FolkInCornwall)

Big thanks to all!

Introduction: The song collectors

Folk music, in its various forms, has always existed. However the term only started being used in the way we would understand it now during the 1800's, as a result of an emerging post-Enlightenment interest in folklore.

Foremost amongst the early folklorists were pioneers like The Brothers Grimm, who collected and recorded folk tales that were part of a German oral story-telling tradition. Across Europe others were inspired by their example and in Cornwall publications by Robert Hunt ('Popular Romances of the West of England') and William Bottrell ('Traditions and Hearthside Stories of West Cornwall') followed in 1865 and 1870 respectively.

Folk songs were collected in much the same way, and one of the first and most celebrated of all the British song collectors lived in Lew Trenchard on the edge of Dartmoor, close to the Cornwall-Devon boundary. Best known by many as the writer of the hymn 'Onward Christian Soldiers', his name was Reverend Sabine Baring-Gould.

Baring-Gould was both parson and squire of Lew Trenchard, and was prolific in many senses of the word: he was an author as well as the father - with his much younger wife - of 17 children.

His 'Songs and Ballads of the West' was first published in 1889, and it is a compilation of musical scores for more than 100 songs collected in Devon and Cornwall.

Baring-Gould and his collaborators are known to have travelled across the region in search of *'old men'* singers over a period of about 10 years. Amongst the better known Cornish music in the collection is 'Sweet Nightingale'; sent by an 'E.F Stevens, Esq of the Terrace, St Ives' and a version of the Helston 'Hal-an-Tow'.

Baring-Gould explains that as the Cornish language died out and became incomprehensible in the 18th Century, English words were grafted onto many preexisting Cornish tunes. So, as is typical of many traditional Cornish songs, whilst the lyrics to Sweet Nightingale were written and sung in London in the 1700's, the tune is uniquely Cornish: one of several '*melodies that probably had accompanied words in the old Cornish tongue in former times. Davey 2007.*

The book is dedicated to one of Baring-Gould's friends, Mr Daniel Radford who, according to the introduction '...*knew that a number of traditional songs and ballads still floated about, and saw clearly that unless these were at once collected they would be lost irretrievably...*'

In explaining why the songs were at risk, Sabine-Gould refers obliquely to the advance of industrialization '*The purely agricultural districts are most auriferous. In manufacturing counties modern music has driven out the traditional folk melodies*'.

Importantly, he also mentions religious music: '*Nowadays, domestic servants sing nothing but hymns...*' and Methodism: '*One of my old singers, James Oliver, was the son of very strict Wesleyans. When he was a boy, he was allowed to hear no music save psalm and hymn tunes.*

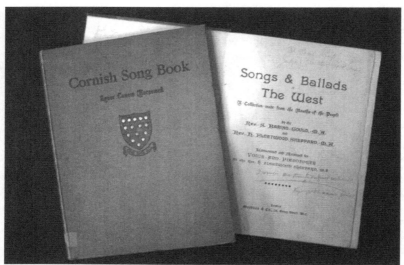

First editions of two of the earliest collections of Cornish folk music

The song-collector's comments about Methodism were echoed by Ralph Dunstan writing in the Cornish Song Book of 1929: *'With the great Wesley Revival a reaction set in against secular songs, and hymns and Christmas Carols took the place of 'the Devil's music''*

Folk singer Brenda Wootton - who, coincidentally, chose a faintly satanic image as the emblem for her folk-club - expressed a similar view nearly 100 years later when she compared folk music in Brittany to that in Cornwall: *'Their music and dance is very strong and wild (of course, Charles Wesley didn't come and save them with his hymns – consequently killing off all the natural local music as in our case).*Cornish Review Spring 1972.

It is undoubtedly the case that for more than a century Methodism shaped much cultural activity in Cornwall, as well as creating significant new cultural forms. The most relevant example of the latter would be the 'tea-treat', comprising Sunday tea taken outdoors by whole communities and here described by Merv Davey: *At the height of its popularity, the Tea Treat involved a procession (or Furry Dance) through the village lead by the local band and decorated with various banners of the organisations involved such as the Band of Hope.*

Some tea-treats incorporated older folk customs, such as the Snail Creep dance: *The Snail Creep...involved a long procession of couples following a band, led by two people holding up branches: the tentacles of the snail. A feature of the custom was the large number of people typically involved, one event in Bugle recorded as many as 600 adults and 350 children participating.*

Dancing was therefore a feature of many tea-treats, but the music played tended to be religious in content: typically Wesleyan hymns, or marches *'which could be played slowly so that the children and old people could keep up.'*(Dunstan)

And the brass bands and male voice choirs which became increasingly popular in Cornwall at the turn of the century, evolved out of this same context. Inevitably they initially retained much of the same repertoire.

In 1890 in an attempt to take traditional folk music to new, larger audiences Sabine Baring-Gould organised for a concert party largely made up of his own family members to visit venues in towns across the

9

South-west. But in fact it was Cecil Sharp, who in founding the Folk Song Society (later the English Folk Dance and Song Society or EFDSS) in 1898, probably did most to organise and promote traditional folk song across England as a whole.

Gorsedd 1929, Carn Brea. Initiated in 1928, and following a surge of interest in the Cornish Language, the Gorsedd was the most visible manifestation of the 'Cornish Revival' of the 20s and 30s

Sharp, who was based in London but involved with extensive song-collecting himself (particularly in Somerset and the Appalachians in the U.S.), visited Baring-Gould in Devon several times in 1904 and 1905. These visits culminated in the revised and final edition of *Songs of the West* and in the book *English Folk Songs for Schools* which he produced in collaboration with Baring-Gould in 1906. In the same year Sharp dedicated his *English Folk Song - Some Conclusions* to Baring-Gould.

Sharp went on to visit Cornwall once in 1913 and twice in 1914 towards the end of his own period of song-collecting. His engagement with the region was in many ways cursory, however, and he has been criticised in some quarters for ignoring Cornwall's celticity. This was true of the EFDSS as a whole which, even via its Cornish branch, had a tendency to promote the Morris dances of the Midlands rather than explore more local traditions (Davey 2012).

Other song-collectors are also known to have been active in Cornwall in the early part of the 20th century. These included George Gardiner and an American by the name of James Madison Carpenter who in 1931 made recordings using a wax cylinder.

The 19th century interest in folklore had led to a fully-fledged 'Cornish Revival' which ran parallel to the activities of the song-collectors, and was supportive of their efforts. In 1904 Henry Jenner, having spent many years working in the British Museum, wrote 'Handbook of the Cornish Language', and successfully applied to the Celtic Congress for Cornwall to be accepted as a Celtic Nation. As well as setting up the Federation of Old Cornwall Societies in 1924, other revivalists like Robert Morton Nance championed symbols of Cornish identity, including tartan and the black and white cross of the St Piran flag.

In this transformative prewar period, the Old Cornwall Societies were instrumental in reviving the 'Crying the Neck' harvest ceremony and the 'Golowan' bonfires. Then 1928 saw the first Cornish Gorsedd (or College of Bards) (see picture).

The event included a song written by Morton Nance, which was published the following year in Ralph Dunstan's 'The Cornish Song Book'. The book contains a collection of around 150 songs, some collected personally by the author, with others taken from the 'Old Cornwall' journal. It includes a separate section of carols including the much-loved 'The Holly and The Ivy'.

After the war, in 1951, Peter Kennedy worked with local singer Charlie Bate, to make a cine film of the 'Obby 'Oss in Padstow, which was released in 1953. Kennedy's father was then director of the EFDSS, and his collaborator on the Padstow project the influential American song collector Alan Lomax, who had recently moved to London.

11

Brenda Wootton and her grandchildren, Davy and Jan, backstage in the early 1980's. Both boys are wearing Cornish tartan and carrying St Piran flags, symbols of the Cornwall which Brenda helped popularise. They called Brenda 'Damawyn' or grandmother.

The narration, provided by Bate, features the words to the Padstow May Day Song and the film, as well having colourful footage of the pageant itself, includes a remarkable black and white sequence of dancers in The Golden Lion the night before (see photo).

Kennedy went on to collect folk song recordings from all over the British Isles to feature on his BBC radio programme 'As I roved out'. In 1956 he visited the Isles of Scilly, and on the mainland recorded Cadgwith fishermen, the Matthew Brothers of Logan Rock, and ensembles such as the 'Truro Wassail Bowl Singers'. He also obtained material, including Cornish language songs, from the 'Skinners Bottom Glee Singers'.

Much of this music was printed later in the Cornish section of his influential compendium '*Folk Songs of Britain and Ireland*' in 1975, some of it also appearing in '*Canow Kernow*', by composer Inglis Gundry (1966).

The activities of the folklorists, folk-song collectors and revivalists in the first half of the Twentieth Century came at a time of increasing financial hardship. Cornwall's mining industry had collapsed - prompting mass migration - and helped by investment by the Great Western Railway, a more modest economy based on tourism was taking its place.

This fledgling industry picked up in the period after the Second World War, as more and more people bought cars. At the time swing or dance bands and solo singers like Doris Day, Frank Sinatra and Vera Lynn dominated the British airwaves and singles charts.

Dancers in The Golden Lion, Padstow the night before May Day, 1951. One is the 'Oss', and the other the 'teaser'. A still from 'Oss Oss Wee Oss.'

Then suddenly in the 1960's, coinciding with Cornwall's increased popularity as a tourist destination, folk music went mainstream. No longer the preserve of the folklorist or musicologist, it was reinvented and became a genre within popular music.

Partly due to the evangelizing efforts of Cecil Sharp's EFDSS, traditional folk song and folk dance were taught in schools in the post-war period and were often featured on the radio. Both helped create an audience receptive to folk. But in the UK it was really the presence of American folk, skiffle, jazz and blues that fuelled the surge in popularity of folk music at the time.

It was a period in history in which vibrant and distinctive new forms of youth culture emerged, many of them borrowing ideas and imagery from the U.S. So it was that in the early 60's, young beatniks 'on the road' came to Cornwall and brought their guitars and their love of American folk and blues music with them.

This American music was originally music of the fields. It spoke of a simple life: of God, farming and the railway and, though estranged from its origins, seemed to find a natural home in this relatively remote and unspoilt part of South West England.

Living in tents, benders, caravans and beach shelters, beatnik musicians like Clive Palmer, Wizz Jones, John the Fish, Ralph McTell, Michael Chapman and Donovan came to adopt Cornwall as their spiritual or actual home. Although initially reviled, and seen as a threat to the tourist economy, their presence, alongside other more local musicians, eventually produced an unusually lively folk-scene.

The folk-scene, as it developed, became an intimately interwoven community, not unlike the artist-colonies Cornwall is already well known for. For those that were involved, music-making and socialising were one and the same thing. Guitarist Pete Berryman has described it as '*a series of circles, or families with the immediate local family based around the clubs in St Buryan and Mitchell and a larger, overlapping, family involving performers on the wider British club circuit*'. Davey 2012.

As an especially creative family, the folk scene in Cornwall produced more than 20 albums of folk music that are still enjoyed today. These albums include some of the most transcendental (COB), popular (Ralph

McTell & Donovan), technically accomplished (Michael Chapman, Wizz Jones and Pete Stanley) and Cornish (Brenda Wootton) folk records of the 20th Century.

One of the first albums of Bluegrass ever recorded by UK-based musicians.
The incongruous cover photo, evocative of the Wild West, was taken in Holywell Bay, Cornwall.

'Folk in Cornwall' is an attempt to describe the context in which those records were made for those, like myself, that were not actually there. I'm indebted to all those who were, who contributed their recollections with such enthusiasm and candour. What has emerged, is I hope, a collective memory of a very particular, and uniquely interesting, moment in time.

Chapter One: Skiffle Gypsies

Subject to a tide-like ebb and flow of summer visitors, the Cornish folk clubs of the 1960's would eventually draw performers and audience members from around the country, each bringing with them their own particular regional accents and influences.

In the late 50's a number of the key protagonists were still teenagers growing up in London, many rubbing shoulders with one another in West End clubs and coffee bars, and in the process picking up on emerging musical trends deriving from the American jazz and folk tradition.

John The Fish holding his first edition (1947) book: 'Best loved American Folk Songs' in 2012. It was one of a number he bought in the West End of London during the late 50's.

John the Fish, or 'Fish', is the affectionate nick-name of John Langford. Later a cornerstone of the Cornish folk scene and accompanist to Brenda Wootton, Fish grew up in North London and played skiffle as a teenager: *We didn't have a television, but we had a radio and my mother used to love singing. She used to persuade me to sing so she could sing harmony with me. I used to listen to 'Two-way family favourites' and 'Housewives Choice'. The pop songs that I remember then were things like The Weavers 'So long it's been good to know you', and Burl Ives 'Big rock candy mountain'.*

Skiffle was played with affordable instruments and needed little in the way of tuition or musical know-how. A relatively obscure genre of music originating in New Orleans, it was revived in the UK in the 1950's. Here it grew out of the developing post-war jazz scene, which had seen a move away from Swing music towards more authentic Trad Jazz. Skiffle was subsequently brought to public attention by Lonnie Donnegan. Starting with 'Rock Island Line', Donnegan, who was a member of the Chris Barber Jazz band, had a series of hit records on both sides of the Atlantic.

John the Fish: *Folk music wasn't something that came into my conscience until I started going to jazz clubs. I used to go to the Wood Green Jazz Club and watch Chris Barber, Kenny Ball and Ken Colyer. Both Ken Colyer and Chris Barber started skiffle groups. It became a craze. Do-it-yourself music. It was through them that I got an interest in music and playing the guitar. A bloke I worked with said 'I'll teach you, but first you should play a ukulele'. He showed me a few chords and things like that. All you needed was three chords for skiffle and then you were away!*

John the Fish soon developed a passion for American folk songs, and whilst living in London bought song books edited by the likes of Pete Seeger and Alan Lomax. Lomax, who worked with Peter Kennedy after moving to the UK, had collected a lot of American Folk music, including blues. Fish: *Alan Lomax collected songs from Leadbelly who at the time was in prison on a manslaughter charge...I didn't read music so mainly used the books for the lyrics.*

Fish also learnt songs by studying 'Sing' magazine. Sing, a folk 'fanzine' with small print-run (less than 1000 per edition), was first printed in 1954 and edited by John Hasted and Eric Winter. Hasted was a professor of Physics who later retired to Cornwall, and sustained a correspondence with Pete Seeger throughout the 1950's. At the time he wrote enthusiastically in support of skiffle.

18

John the Fish's 1957 copy of Sing magazine. Inside the front cover are the words and tune to 'This Land is My Land' by Woody Guthrie, as performed by 'cowboy' Jack Elliott.

John the Fish subsequently brought his music books to Cornwall with him, and shared them with others, including Brenda Wootton.

Singer and banjo-player Clive Palmer was a founder member of The Incredible String Band that, in 1969, played at the celebrated Woodstock festival. As we shall see, Clive went on to make several highly-regarded folk albums with musicians that he met in Cornwall.

Like Fish he started out playing guitar in a skiffle band in the mid 1950's in North London: *I had a skiffle band with some friends and a guitar that my brother did up. Then I met someone who had a banjo - an old one in a case - and we swapped. I just liked the look of it more than a guitar! I got a few books, then went to the library. They said there was a banjo club, which were all over the country at one time. I was introduced to a teacher, Alfred Lloyd, who was about the best player of the day. I was lucky. I happened to be in the right place at the right time...*

19

We got on the Carroll Levis show at the Finsbury Park Empire. They were live concerts and we had to get a special license because of our age from the council!

Rather than being confined to London the skiffle bug infected every town and village in Britain. Seventies folk-rock star Michael Chapman, who became a regular performer in Cornwall, lived in Leeds as a young teenager. Michael: *I was in a skiffle band at Grammar school. There were 5 of us in the group – 3 acoustic guitars, a tea-chest bass and a washboard. My guitar was only £6 and the tea-chest and washboard cost nothing, so it was the cheapest band on earth. That's why they were so popular: any bunch of lads could have a band. We played at the Youth Club, and we played at the Methodist chapel dances, then, when I went to art college in Leeds, we started to play in pubs.*

Even in the most rural corners of Cornwall, youngsters were inspired to pick up musical instruments. John Sleep, who later founded The Folk Cottage club outside Truro, grew up in Gunnislake, a village in the Tamar Valley close to the Devon border. John: *Everything started with Lonnie Donnegan. His type of music was the first thing that a group of youngsters who couldn't play very well could actually manage. We started a little skiffle group up in Gunnislake, and we used to play at church meetings and dances in Plymouth, even though we were rubbish! Terrible!*

There's such a lot available to listen to now but the only stuff we had to listen to was then was Burl Ives and skiffle. There weren't any good music programmes on the radio in the 50's. Skiffle was verging on blues, and if we'd known what blues was, and how to play it, we'd have definitely gone for that too!

There were several well-publicised skiffle competitions held in Cornwall in the late 50's, and when skiffle died out, it left in its wake a generation of youngsters who continued their music-making into the next decade.

John Sleep, who was one of them, went on to discover an important pioneer of folk music based in Plymouth. His name was Cyril Tawney: *I was 17 or 18 - just old enough to drive - at the time. I used to drive to Plymouth to sing in a folk club with Cyril Tawney who was a wonderful singer. He had a club on The Hoe, in the West Hoe Hotel. He used another venue at Meavy near Yelverton too. He was one of the first and best folk singers in the South West.*

Rosemary Tawney was Cyril's wife: *John is referring to the Plymouth Folk Song Club (PFSC) which, fairly early in its career, was held at the West Hoe Hotel. Cyril's Plymouth clubs were always called PFSC, not by the name of the venue.*

Cyril Tawney's interest in British folk music had, in the early 50's, been stimulated by Peter Kennedy's radio programme. Rosemary: *Alan Lomax began his song-collecting in Britain, which inspired the BBC to commence a five-year collecting campaign of its own, with a weekly shop-window programme on Sunday mornings called 'As I Roved Out'.*

Cyril was unusual in being a song-writer and many of his songs, like 'Sally Free and Easy' later recorded by the likes of Davy Graham, Marianne Faithful and Bob Dylan, were written in the late 50's whilst he was still serving in the Navy. John Sleep: *Cyril was a submariner and he wrote some very good songs. I was very friendly with him, and I sang with him, and I regret that I didn't pursue this friendship. I used to go to the Sidmouth Folk Festival and sing there, and I learnt a lot of his songs.*

In 1959 Cyril bought himself out of the Navy, in order to become a professional singer. His extensive radio and TV work, gained through contact with Lomax and Kennedy, preceded the wide-spread emergence of folk clubs and continued into the sixties when he was given his own BBC programme called 'Folkspin'.

A folk newsletter held in the EFDSS archive, and published by Cyril Tawney, indicates that his subsequent attempts to start up a local club were not very successful: '*When the club first opened at the Plymouth Inn, Plympton, in January 1962, we came almost to a standstill after four or five months because we couldn't get people to travel out from Plymouth. Attendances dropped to about half-a-dozen or so. Consequently we moved into Plymouth*'.

The club moved several times. As well as West Hoe Hotel, other venues included Lower Guildhall, Plymouth (1963), Eggbuckland Keep (1964), and Barn Dances at Cornwood Public Hall and Meavy Village Hall.

Rosemary explains: *Cyril had a great deal of regional TV and radio work in the first half of the '60s so he was around much more than he was later on. He opened the West of England Folk Centre in 1965 and after that had little spare time. When not on tour, he had to concentrate on keeping the Centre going.*

Cyril Tawney performing at The Count House c1965. He wrote some of the best-loved songs of the 60's folk revival eg 'Sally Free and Easy' as recorded by Bob Dylan (photo John the Fish).

Folk music in the provinces was still under the influence of Cecil Sharp's EFDSS. John Sleep: *At University I was involved with the EFDSS, but I used to run a folk-dancing club in Launceston. We used to go to leaders courses, which were aimed at people who ran the clubs. I was mainly taught how to call dances.*

In contrast, musicians like John the Fish and Clive Palmer in London were exposed to more and more blues and American music. Fish: *I did National Service between '54 and '56. It was 56 - 57 that I went to the Skiffle Cellar, and Alexis Korner's Barrelhouse and Blues club at the*

Round House, and Bunjies. It was there that I remember Ramblin' Jack Elliott.

Jack travelled with Woody Guthrie, and actually introduced Bob Dylan to Woody Guthrie. Guthrie said 'Jack Elliot is more like Woody Guthrie than I am!' He electrified me really because he played, sung and told stories. He could go on for hours on end, and have a whole audience spell-bound. One man doing that: I thought it was magic. I wanted a basin full of that!

Alexis Korner, Ramblin' Jack Elliott and Big Bill Broonzy in Korners flat 1958 (photo Eric Winter & Ian Anderson)

Elliott, a key figure who linked US and UK folk scenes, was the son of a Brooklyn doctor: yet his stage persona was that of a country cowboy: *In fact it turned out his name was Elliott Adnopoz. All these heroes turn out to be straw men really. So Jack Elliott was an actor more than a singer. He fell into the part: And it was that which inspired me to play solo.*

In 1956, Johnny Booker took over as manager of the Gyre and Gimble all-night coffee bar (also known as 'the G's') and began to play music there with friends who became the nucleus of The Vipers, one of the foremost bands in the 1950's skiffle scene. They had a number of hit records, with Booker (recording as 'Johnny Martyn') as one of the singers.

1956 was also the year that Clive Palmer's mother died. He was only 13 at the time. Shortly after this he became a regular visitor to the G's, and would often end up sleeping rough in the West End. Clive: *The Gyre and Gimble was on the Strand, and I used to cycle in there from where I was living. I was still at school, but I was mixing with a lot of musicians. People like Davy Graham, Rod Stewart and Long John Baldry. We used to spend the night there, sometimes all night just playing, like round-robin. Everyone would just have a go, sort of thing.*

Kazoo players in The Partisan Coffee House, 1960. Long John Baldry is the seated guitar player
(photo Ian Anderson & Eric Winter)

Long John Baldry was an important pioneer of blues who in the sixties formed bands that included Mick Jagger, Rod Stewart and Elton John as backing musicians. He would later accompany guitar pioneer Wizz Jones to Newquay in Cornwall. Wizz Jones: *I first glimpsed sight of John on Charing Cross Station in 1957. He was carrying a guitar with 'Long John' painted in white across the case. I subsequently got to know him and busk with him a few times under the arches at Charing Cross (across from the 'Gyre and Gimble'). He was truly a profound influence on the budding young Blues guitar crowd at that time.*

Soon-to-be English pop star Tommy Steele was another visitor to the G's, as was artist and Situationist Ralph Rumney who, incidentally, earlier in the 50's lived in St Ives as Barbara Hepworth's assistant.

Clive Palmer remembers other London clubs: *The all night club was Ken Colyer's. Then there was Russell Quaye's Skiffle Cellar, The Partisan Coffee House in Soho and Ewan McColl's club, The Singer's Club which was purely traditional. And there were people like Seamus Ennis playing around the Irish clubs in Kilburn.*

The Partisan is now also remembered as a meeting place of the new left: a place where CND was founded and where politics and music were brought together, most notably in the LP 'Songs against the Bomb', recorded there in 1960.

Chapter two: King of the beatniks

Wizz Jones had grown up in Croydon where he started playing with his band The Wranglers in 1957. *I had this little skiffle group and we were really playing country music - Hank Williams stuff - and we'd get gigs playing at the cinemas before Elvis Presley films.*

After moving out of his parent's house and finding a job in London, he was inspired to start playing solo blues guitar: *I'd heard it on the radio on the BBC Third Programme. But it was through going to jazz clubs and seeing Jesse Fuller and Big Bill Broonzy that I really discovered that music. I also saw Muddy Waters, Ramblin' Jack Elliott and Derroll Adams playing in Alexis Korner's Barrelhouse and Blues club in 1958. It was a tiny little place but many of the people in that audience went on to become well-known musicians.*

Wizz also learnt from his contemporaries: *There were a set of people 8 or 9 years older than me. People like Steve Benbow, Alexis Korner and Cyril Davis, but my real peers were Davy Graham and Long John Baldry and a couple of other people. They were the only people around doing it then, so in the winter in London I'd busk with Long John sometimes and with Davy, the three of us. They were younger than me, slightly, but they were still ahead of me musically, and they helped turned me on to it all. I was lucky to be in Soho then, but actually I think it was also happening independently in Edinburgh and Liverpool and places like that.*

Singer-songwriter Ralph McTell: *Wizz was turning into the obligatory beatnik dropout, having given up on a boring warehouse job in The City. For many he was a role model - not just the way he dressed and played, but where he had travelled and the means by which he got there. Wizz's guitar was also a little unusual - he had discovered the legendary handmade La Foley in 1959 at the Lew Davis guitar shop in Charing Cross Road. It was priced at twenty pounds and Wizz was allowed five pounds part-exchange for his Hofner Zenith.* 16 Tons

Wizz on Great Western beach, Newquay. Photo by life guard Roy Heath

Wizz: *We got labeled 'beatniks'. In the 50's Britain was so gloomy. Everyone wore trilby hats, grey flannel trousers and collar and ties. You'd get on a tube train and it would be full of these boring people, but right at the end of the carriage you'd see a girl in black stockings or a bloke with long hair and you'd go over and talk to them.*

It was only a way of trying to find something different from our boring, horrible working class backgrounds. Which led to that creative scene where everyone rubbed shoulders with everybody else. You had working class kids and public school boys all thrown together in the melting pot which was wonderful. Since the drink- driving laws people don't congregate in Soho as they used to but when we were growing up people came in from far and wide. We were very lucky.

In Soho, Cornwall came to acquire a reputation amongst this generation of young, pioneering musicians. Wizz Jones: *I first went busking in Cornwall in the summer of 1959. Malcolm Price went down in 1958.*

27

*We were all hanging around in Soho and people there used to say
'We're either going to France or going to Cornwall'. I went to
Cornwall first before I went to France.*

Malcolm Price's guitar technique had been learnt from Ramblin' Jack
himself. Wizz: *When Jack came to London, it was like the Messiah
arriving. After he left, I remember Malcolm Price buying a guitar and
learning to do that same flat-picking style. He was the first that I ever
met in London that could do it – he did it in a few weeks, sat and
practiced all night, and he was our absolute champion.*

Malcolm was probably the first beatnik guitarist to visit Cornwall: *He
squatted in Rose Cottage in Heligan Woods (in mid-Cornwall). Hew
Weldon made a programme called Monitor and they filmed Malcolm in
the cottage but unfortunately the BBC wiped it which was a great
shame.*

*Malcolm was really the first guy to go down to Cornwall with an
acoustic guitar. In those days there were a few jazz combos with people
playing electric organs, and a few rock and roll bands like 'Cousin
Jacks'. But it wasn't till Malcolm came down and started to play
acoustic folk guitar that it started to happen.*

28

Ralph McTell: *Malcolm lived in a deserted game-keeper's cottage which was a squat. He was there with his runaway teenage girlfriend encamped in the woods at the bottom of the Heligan estate. Malcolm was one of the finest flat-picking guitar players I'd ever heard. When I saw him in folk clubs later, he was also very funny and witty.*

Wizz: *So the blues thing didn't really happen in Cornwall, but there was a healthy New Orleans traditional jazz scene all over the country in the 50's, even though it had started out as quite alternative and underground - as folk did. There were hardly any folk clubs then. In 1959 there was only The Topic in Bradford and Ewan McColl's lot in London and maybe the Spinners in Liverpool. But that was it. There wasn't really a network. It took two or three years to really explode.*

When I first got to Cornwall in 1959 the Newquay Jazz club was happening in a church hall in Crantock Street, and there was also a Jazz Club in St Austell. I remember going to a jazz club when Malcolm and Carol got up and played in the interval.

Wizz had hitched to Cornwall with songwriter Alan Tunbridge, with whom he would collaborate for the next 20 or more years. Alan: *I first encountered Wizz in 1958, in 'The Partisan' coffee bar, Soho - and later we occasionally met at 'The House of Sam Widges' and other Soho hangouts. I was thunderstruck when I first heard him playing at the Partisan. He wasn't performing, just practicing at a corner table.*

In early spring of 1959 I heard that a group of beats planned to hitch down to Newquay and decided to join them. I quit my job at an Argyle Street ad agency and hitched down the A30. Shortly after arrival we heard that The Bredon Court Hotel was taking on staff, so a group of us applied and landed jobs. Wizz and I and a couple of others were in the plate room. We all slept in a staff dormitory.

Wizz taught me a few guitar chords. When I'd mastered the first three, I did a little tune for Edgar Allen Poe's poem 'The Raven'. Wizz thought it had merit, and played it with lots more chords and fiddly bits thrown in. I was hooked. When I got back to London I bought myself a guitar and started tinkering with words and music. Every time I finished a song I would play it into a tape recorder and send the tape to Wizz, who would play it in folk clubs. Later he included the songs on his albums.

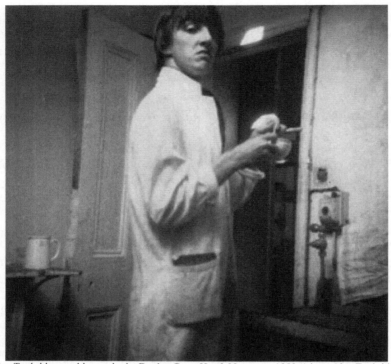

Alan Tunbridge washing up in the Bredon Court Hotel, Newquay. 1959. (photo Alan Tunbridge)

Guitarist Pete Berryman was a few years younger than Wizz. Living in Newquay at the time, he now remembers the beatniks from Soho with some fondness: *Newquay was a very small place then and everybody knew the beatniks. There was Wizz 'King of the Beatniks' and Mad Eric who was a shuffling person with a long army coat who never washed, and various others.*

I remember that during my school holiday I sold ice cream in a little stationary ice cream van on the Active Cellar (pilchard cellar) which is the other side of the harbour and they used to crash out in the cellar. In fact I remember seeing a really lanky guy in a long leather coat in there one day and I realise now that it was Long John Baldry because he was one of that clique as well. So they'd be hanging around and I'd give them free ice-creams. And Wizz always had a guitar strung on his back and I can remember him playing it.

Jimmy Rogers who was a mentor to my band was a member of that clique, and so was his brother who was called 'John the Bomb'. There were other guys like 'Swearing Chas' who is a business man in Newquay now...

Alan Tunbridge also remembers six-foot-seven Long John Baldry in Newquay in 1959. Alan: *My memory of him is of how truly weird he looked in beat garb - like something imagined by Lewis Carroll. The sheer size of his fishbelly-white sandaled feet is indelibly branded on my memory!*

Wizz playing in the Beresford Hotel near Great Western beach September 1959 with Ron Keys on banjo. Ron Keys later played with The Wurzels (photo: wizzjones.com)

Wizz: *Long John came down to Newquay in 1959, when we were all working in hotels. I remember we dressed Long John up and used Evostick on his face to make loads of fake scars and he went down and terrorised some of the guys in the tents...*

In 1969 Wizz Jones asked Long John to write the sleeve-notes for one of his LP's. He took it as an opportunity to add yet more to the extraordinary role-call of beat nick-names: *Listening to this album takes me back through many years, many memories of long hot summers in Newquay and milk trains to Brighton for Sunday raves on the front. Of*

31

afternoons in Sam Widges, Soho and nights at the Gyre and Gimble Charing Cross. Of long-disappeared friends and half-forgotten faces - Iron foot Jack, Swearing Chas, John the Dragon, Countess Irene, Kind David, Princess Sheba, Iris Onion, Ernest Page the Astrologer, Poochie and Alan Tunbridge and Wizz Jones....

Wizz on the steps above Great Western Beach, Newquay.

Clive Palmer, another of the Soho beats, also came to Newquay in 1959: *We came down first to Cornwall and played in the streets. We busked in Newquay, and then went to Paris after that.*

Alan: *Most of my 1959 group had accommodation in their employing hotels and were usually well behaved, but there were a few stragglers passing through who occasionally caused some alarm. I remember one, known as 'Black Roger', who frightened some families on the beach by picking up a dead fish and eating it raw!*

32

*Then there was the 'happening' we staged in the local Woolworths:
Wizz pretended to be fishing down a road-drain outside, a white van
screeched to a halt and white-coated figures (beats who were in on the
act) jumped out to chase Wizz noisily around the crowded store. All
would have gone well if some overenthusiastic pursuer had not collided
with a kid in a wheelchair on the pavement outside!*

Wizz and his friends whiled away many hours on the beaches. Wizz:
*We used to go along to Western. We always used to meet there. We'd
also meet on 'The Cove' which has fallen away now, which was past the
harbour by the fly cellars.*

*Roy Heath the lifeguard took that photo of me sitting on a rock on
Western beach. In 1959 I got to know a few guys that were working as
lifeguards and they had all just got into surfing. They were bums - not
working - just living to ride the waves - and we were living by busking
and playing music and in that sense we were kindred spirits.*

Two of the same lifeguards have since entered surfing history: *Doug
opened the first surf factory - Bilbo - with Bill Bailey. They were the
first people to make Malibu surfboards in Europe. Bill Bailey was a
lifeguard on Western, Doug was a lifeguard on Fistral, Bob Head was a
lifeguard on Towan. A lot of the lifeguards had friends who worked in
the hotels, and they would come down and bring coffee and food down
from the hotels. It was a real bum lifestyle!*

It was a lifestyle that was met with disapproval by parts of the business
community in Newquay, however, and the unruly presence of the
beatniks came to be seen as a threat to the tourist economy.
Wizz: *In '59 we could get work in the hotels because the big furor
hadn't started. But the next year as so often happens - it happened in
Paris - lots of people follow you over - lots of hangers-on and lots of
dodgy people that fuck it up for everybody else. That's what happened
in 1960, and that's what happened in St Ives the following year with
Donovan and all that lot.*

So it was that in 1960 many of the shops and bars refused to serve them,
and were supported in this by the council. Ralph McTell: *The skiffle
gypsies, as the locals had called them were being superseded by
undesirable beatniks, such as Wizz and his friends. Things reached such
a fever pitch that Alan Whicker was sent down to film interviews with*

councillors, hoteliers and beatniks on the banks of the River Gannel in
Newquay where Wizz and his crowd were camping. 16tons

Hard Times in Newquay: Wizz Jones filmed by the BBC in 1960 on the River Gannel in Newquay

The recently rediscovered film, originally made for the BBC's
'Tonight' programme, opens with the 21 year old Wizz Jones singing
imploringly to the camera:

Come you ladies and gentleman listen to my song
I'll sing it to you right but you may think it's wrong
If you want to hear more then listen to me
It's all about the troubles in old Newquay
'Cos it's hard times in Newquay if you've got long hair

You move into old Newquay
then you pitch your tent by the sea
then along come the law and they move you away
'Cos the urban district council don't want you to stay
'Cos it's hard times in Newquay if you've got long hair
Well you smarten up and put on some shoes,
try and get a job to drive away the blues
but everywhere you go they stand and stare,
and can't employ you because you've got long hair
'Cos it's hard times in Newquay if you've got long hair

Take a little train it ain't no sin
but there ain't a pub in Newquay that'll let me in
I search the cafes for a place to eat
but they can't serve you cos you're a beat
'Cos it's hard times in Newquay if you've got long hair

Narrating over images of a small group of long-haired boys and barefoot girls, reporter Alan Whicker continues: *'Hard times indeed for the few remaining beatniks still holding out in this Cornish stronghold against a very determined council that has taken quite unusual steps to drive out its long-haired visitors'*.

One of the town councillors tries to defend himself: *'The trouble started last summer when the first invasion of these types came along. One didn't object to their eccentricities of dress or their long hair, but when it came to forgetting to wash, and becoming dirtier and dirtier and eventually becoming filthy, and finally stinking we felt it was more that we could stand...'*

Wizz: *Actually Alan Whicker himself was very sympathetic; the councillors took us aside and tried to bribe us into not saying too much, which we turned down. I was a stupid kid, well I was 21, but I wasn't very mature, and I thought I was the bee's knees. I was talking to Alan Whicker: 'Yeah man, Jack Kerouac, On the Road!', which I'd read..... And Alan said: 'Yes, On the Road, and there are also some wonderful passages in Dharma Bums too.' I hadn't read that, but he had!*

Alan Tunbridge: *The Newquay 'incident' reported by Whicker was a local phenomenon triggered by increased numbers of 'beats' hitching down to Cornwall in the year after I was there. The Council feared the influx would adversely affect tourist numbers.*

Though recreational drugs later became a feature of beat culture, in the UK in 1959 they were n't. Alan: *To my knowledge Wizz never used drugs of any kind - other than the occasional beer. Not even cigarettes - in an epoch when smoking was universal. When we were hanging out in Soho during the late 50's, no one was using street drugs because they were simply unavailable. It was in the early 60's when cannabis, hashish and speed began to appear in London beat hangouts - but even then pretty rarely. My first contact with this trend was around 1963, when someone showed me how to crack open the plastic tube of a Benzedrine inhaler and swallow a piece of the wadding inside.*

Punk legend Ian Dury visiting beatnik friends camping on the banks of The Gannel c1959. His grandparents lived in Cornwall, and he was staying with them in Mevagissey - as he often did - when he first developed the symptoms of polio as a seven year old in 1949. He was admitted to hospital in Truro City, where he lay paralysed for more than a month. (photo wizzjones.com)

Susie Smith, the tallest of the barefoot teenagers in the film, was at art school in Walthamstow. Susie first met Wizz Jones in the West End: *I went to Newquay about 3 years running probably 1960, 61, '62. There was a whole crowd who came down together - we were friends from the Duke of York pub in Rathbone Street, and Finch's in Goodge Street, and the coffee shops. He was fatherly, and very kind to me. Wizz was such an influential person and so well thought of. There are lots of biographies that mention him. Rod Stewart said Wizz helped him in Paris, Keith Richards mentions Wizz, and Eric Clapton.*

A music lesson on the clifftop with banjo player 'Cousin Will'.

Along the River Gannel there were places to pitch tents, like near the Gannel Boatyard, and most of us had tents. Then if we walked up the hill into Newquay there was a camp site on Tregunnel Hill and we'd go in there and have a shower.

We became known as the Black Mass because everybody wore black clothing! Tourists used to come and look at us like we were wild animals!

Walking along the high street in Newquay people would say things like 'When did you last have a bath?' - just horrible things - pathetic really. People wouldn't serve us in the pubs, but I got a job washing up in a hotel and they were nice and used to feed me. I'd be living in the tent and walk into Newquay to go to work.

Ralph: *When Wizz came to Cornwall he was taken to court for stealing a tuppenny bar of soap out of the gents toilets in Newquay. That's how reactionary people were.*

Another musician who would later have a number one record passed through the community of beatniks. Like Clive Palmer and Donovan he had contracted polio as a boy, and had one leg weaker than the other. Wizz: *Ian Dury had relations in Cornwall. We knew him from London. We knew him as Toulouse when he was at art school with Susie. I remember I was cooking a fish on the side of The Gannel and I saw Ian walking down, wobbling down, the river towards me. And I thought 'what's he's doing here?'*

Busking under Pont Des Arts, Paris 1960. L to R sandy Jones, unknown, Wizz Jones, Clive Palmer, Mick Softley. (photo wizzjones.com)

Wizz and Clive busking in 1961. Carrefour De L'Odeon, Paris. (Photo WizzJones.com)

Some of the beatnik musicians were more accomplished than others. Wizz: *There was a burgeoning interest in acoustic folk stuff and I was playing some 5 string banjo as well as guitar and people were coming to me asking for lessons. Cousin Will learnt to play reasonably well. He was a laugh. He didn't persevere or become professional but it was part of a right of passage with all that lot. They all had a go.*

Wizz's adventures were not confined to Cornwall. Clive Palmer was still at art school in Hornsey when he first went busking in France with Wizz in 1960.

Clive: *I was coming towards the end of the course. I met Wizz outside The Partisan and he said 'I'm going off to Paris busking' and I said 'what's it like?' and he said 'yeh it's great', I so I said 'alright then'. There was another girl who played banjo called Maria and we all went on the train. It was cheap. £12 or something. We arrived in Paris and we got to Saint Germain and we played in front of the café's and made a fortune: £100 in today's money in a couple of hours. So we booked a couple of rooms in a hotel.*

39

Wizz and I went busking all over Paris. We did it for two or three years: 59, 60, 61. Other musicians went over there, like Alex Campbell, Davy Graham and Martin Windsor. We all used to stay together quite a lot and meet up in the same cafe called the Monaco Bar.

Wizz with wife-to-be Sandy on the banks of The Gannel. 1961.

We'd play the whole winter. Wizz eventually went off on his own. He went down South (in France) and tried it alone. Then I ran into trouble. I'd been there for so long that my visa had expired, and De Gaule was kicking out itinerant artists and musicians.

Wizz returned to Cornwall for long periods over successive summers: *In 1961, having done a bit of travelling I spent time hanging around and busking with my girlfriend Sandy. There was still no folk scene as such then. I was again camping down by the Gannel. In 1962 we were out of the country most of the time, travelling down to Morocco. When we came back - after spending the winter in Paris - in 1963, we went to Cornwall and worked picking potatoes and working in cafes. I worked in a cafe called The Sandcrest which is now an Indian Restaurant up the top near the Great Western Hotel. I worked in there washing up and playing guitar in the evenings 2 or 3 times a week.*

Chapter Three: Beat journeys

The term 'Beat Generation' was first coined by the writer Jack Kerouac in the late 40's to refer to a group of anti-establishment writers who became an important rallying-point for the emerging counter-culture of the sixties.

In the UK the beats as a subculture soon came to be seen as sub-versives, and, with liberal and left-wing sympathies, they were closely allied to the emerging Campaign for Nuclear Disarmament (CND). Susie Smith: *There were all the Aldermaston Marches and we all went on them all the time. I went on about 4. Rod Stewart went on one. I used to go with Ian Dury. It's amazing he used to go considering his bad leg. He had a caliper, and we'd have to carry him sometimes.*

Wizz Jones: *We were very idealistic. We sang the songs about Nagasaki and knew about the bomb. A lot of the people we admired, like Spike Milligan of The Goons and Bertrand Russell were extreme left-wing. We didn't really know what we were doing, we just wanted something to believe in.*

Rod Stewart said 'you went on the Aldermaston March because it was so free and easy'. They opened all the schools and every night you got to crash out on the floor in the school and it was mixed young girls and young boys! So yeh we wanted to ban the bomb, but we were also up for the crack.

I got to know Rod when he was in his Mod period. He used to drink in The Finches and play his harmonica – he'd sit at one end of the table and me at the other end. He never busked with me, though he has claimed to have done, but he did come to Paris when I was there.

Wizz Jones in Trafalgar Square, 1960. The guitar, which is not his own, is painted with peace signs. (photo wizzjones.com)

Often also caricatured as work-shy dropouts or vagrants, the beatniks became the subject of a number of sensational B-movies and, for example, were blamed in the tabloid press for riots at the Beaulieu Jazz Festival of 1960 (see picture).

Alan Tunbridge: *It's difficult these days for anyone under 60 to imagine what society was like for young people in Britain during the 40s/50s. Only wealthy people had TV, and everyone appearing on it was middle-aged and wore evening dress. 'Pop music' was cheesy Doris Day ballads or infantile novelty songs. No one under 30 appeared in movies - except as outright children. It was as if teenagers did not exist, and indeed it took the invention of the term 'teenagers' to bring them into media existence. Consequently the development of a teenage subculture bent on getting noticed as rebels against the culture which ignored them was inevitable.*

Alan highlights a book that was an important influence on this emerging youth culture. Its author had moved to Cornwall himself in the late 50's: *Colin Wilson's 'Outsider' certainly reflected the social alienation experienced by some young people. It associated youth's*

43

instinctive rejection of the status quo with such established 'heroes' as Camus, Hesse, Sartre, etc. Colin Wilson was received by intellectually-inclined Beats as an additional endorsement of their wish to reject all prescribed behaviours and to 'hit the road down South'. As such, it was certainly one of the influencers which encouraged me to quit my job and hitch down to Newquay with £5 and Omar's Rubáiyát in my duffel bag.

Somehow this literary affiliation came to be symbolised by wearing long hair, self-tailored drainpipe corduroy trousers, long black sweaters, and either 'desert' boots or 'Jesus' sandals. By today's standards of youth fashion the look was innocuous, but in those days passing traffic would slow down for a closer look.

'Blame these 4 men for the Beatnik horror'. People on Sunday. Kerouac ('the hobo's prophet'), Corso ('the crank poet'), Burroughs ('the ex-drug addict') and Ginsberg ('the hate merchant') are blamed for the violence at the Beaulieu Jazz Festival in 1960: 'The four beatnik prophets do not themselves preach violence. But they do infect their followers with indifference or outright hostility to established codes of conduct'

And it was the media who called us 'beatniks': we disdained all such limiting tags! Wizz Jones was an extreme example with his penchant for hand-glued leather patches on everything - even his guitar and spectacles - but others adopted other styles.

44

Clive Palmer: *There were the beatniks and there were the smoothies who wore suits. They were the modern jazz crowd. Rod Stewart was a mod. Davy Graham was part of that set, too, not so much part of the folkie-beatnik thing.*

'We do everything, feel everything strictly for kicks': 'Beat Girl' 1959, stars Adam Faith, Christopher Lee and Oliver Reed. Here, Jenny, the middle-class teenager at the centre of the drama, sneaks out of her house to visit a late-night coffee bar in Soho.

Alan describes the beats he knew in Soho and Newquay: *Musically, the group favoured traditional jazz, and most were habitués of the Cy Laurie club in Shaftsbury Avenue, London. Elvis had recorded 'Heartbreak Hotel' in 1956, and in 1959 Cliff Richard's 'Living Doll' was permanently playing on every jukebox in England, but we generally cleaved to old jazz and other folk music, snobbishly rejecting any new wave as 'populist'. Along with our semi-bizarre clothes, these music preferences further distinguished us from the prevalent youth culture: the 'Mods'. While most other teenagers were vigorously aiding the birth of Rock and the future 60's revolution, my subgroup unwittingly belonged to the movement which would produce such folky/blues exponents as Bob Dylan, Martin Carthy, Joan Baez, The Pentangle, Wizz Jones and others.*

Singer-songwriter Ralph McTell also identified strongly with the beat movement: *I had a bit of a troubled childhood. And like many boys who come from broken homes I had a dodgy early teenage period until I discovered music. I properly discovered roots in American music when I was about 16. I fell in with the beatnik crowd in Croydon where I lived. The four beatniks I knew were all a couple of years older than me. There was nowhere to go, but some of these fellers got themselves a little flat and I spent hours round there listening to Art Blakey and Miles Davis and people like that.*

After abandoning religion and conventional ways of going about things, I became interested in alternative beatnik cultures revealing all the mysteries of life. Beat culture was education out of school. You would ponder the poems, and the stories and the flow-of- consciousness stuff. And Bob Dylan was a student of that stuff, so when we heard Dylan we got him too. It was going on in other cities at the same time: Liverpool, Glasgow and Dublin. The whole culture gave us an identity, and a discipline, and a more enquiring mind.

Wizz Jones: *It was romantic. You read Jack Kerouac and thought 'Yeah, that's great, I wanna do that'. And possibly for all the wrong reasons. I mean I used to think that I was very politically motivated and idealistic, but to be honest, most of the time I was probably just doing it for the fun of it.* ptolemeic terrascope

The figure of Woody Guthrie, who had helped inspire the skiffle craze in the UK, also loomed large over the 60's folk revival. As an inspiration he was as important as any of the beat writers. Ralph: *My mentor by this time was Woody Guthrie who'd done the travelling for socialist reasons: he was a committed Union man. It was a combination of a political view, music, poetry and guitar playing. Woody's message better served my purposes rather than Jack Kerouac's which was more modern jazz though I took that on board as well.*

In the early sixties, like Wizz Jones and Clive Palmer, Ralph McTell went busking all over the world. Ralph: *My Dad was in the desert rats and had been abroad during the war, but none of the rest of my family had even thought of travelling. We hitchhiked everywhere because it was 'noble'. You took the rough with the smooth. Boys had to wait for hours, girls could go anywhere in comparative safety. Hitchhiking wasn't frowned upon. You were taking a chance. You didn't know if you*

46

would get there, and who you would meet. We'd say things like 'I'll see you in Trieste' and it would take as long as it took to get there. I got as far as Istanbul and would have gone further but I got ill.

I didn't even know where I was going. I bought a map that cost sixpence and by the time I got to the South of France it was in about eight pieces. 'No money in my pocket, a cigarette in my mouth, no fixed destination but some vague direction south'. I had no wish to sit on the beach. I wanted to keep rolling on and playing my guitar. Earning money by busking. I had a ten shilling note when I left England and a ten shilling note when I came back...

The ISB were pioneers of what is now often called Psychfolk. A big influence on many of their peers, including Lennon and McCartney, in 1969 they played at the Woodstock Festival. Clive Palmer is on the left.

Wizz Jones' busking partner, Clive Palmer - like Wizz - travelled extensively in the 60's, and in 1963 moved up to Edinburgh. Once there

47

he made an immediate impression, and found himself in illustrious company. Clive: *Someone said 'the Crown Bar round the corner runs a folk club you should go and play'. So I went round there and met Archie Fisher who ran it and did a spot playing the banjo. They were all amazed - thought it was fantastic.*

After I played this guy came up to me. It was Robin Williamson. Bert Jansch (Pentangle) was there that night as well - he played there regularly. I started chatting with Robin. He said 'I've been doing a lot on my own. I wonder if you'd be interested in playing with me and we could have a duo'. And I said 'sure'. So off we went as Robin and Clive and got loads of work travelling all over Britain: Scotland, the Midlands, Manchester, Sheffield, Birmingham - all them places. Robin was singing ordinary traditional songs but with beautiful arrangements and it was absolutely spellbinding. To me now that was his best time.

Robin and Clive did n't have an agent: *In those days you did it with a postcard. The club would write to you and say 'would you do a gig on the 20th June?' and you'd send back the postcard saying you would. The folk club circuit was really beginning to boom then. We used to get about £60 for a gig for two of us. That was a lot of money. To give you an idea, in 1974 when I worked in a picture framer's in London I was only earning £30 a week.*

Clive went on to share digs with Robin and Bert, and to run his own club in Scotland: *It was in Glasgow. It was the first all-night folk club. It only lasted 6 months before the police closed it down though.*

In 1965 Robin and Clive formed one of the most influential bands of the sixties: The Incredible String Band: *We were stuck in a groove of being a folk duo. We were quite good, and went down a bomb. But we decided to expand it and take on a guitarist. So Mike Heron joined us.*

I met an American lady (Mary Stewart) who had a house out of Glasgow. So I ended up living there for a while and that's when Joe Boyd came along. He knocked on the door one morning and said 'I've heard about your band and I wondered if you fancied making a record'. I said 'what kind of deal is it?' We looked at the paperwork and agreed to go to London and make the first Incredible String Band record.

The studio was Sound Techniques, the famous one in Chelsea. It was a record made in two days. They were almost all first takes. Joe is very good at getting the best out of people: a great catalyst sort of person.

In London Wizz Jones, having lost touch with Clive, had formed a duo with a different banjo-player: Pete Stanley. Pete, who was another regular at the Gyre and Gimble, had taken up banjo playing in 1957 after finishing his national service and finding an old banjo in his parent's attic. He had met Wizz originally at Peggy Seeger's banjo classes in the West End. Pete: *They were small groups with 4 or 5 in a class. Peggy did up-picking – two finger picking – in a boom-ticker rhythm.*

Though the classes only ran for a few weeks, Pete learnt fast, and when Peggy had to return to the States he took her place as the tutor: *I'd been playing banjo for about 6 weeks, and was only one week ahead of my pupils!*

As well as learning from Peggy, Pete listened to records from the American Embassy. *It had a great record library. I borrowed the Harry Smith Anthology, lots of blues records, and stuff by Jack Elliott.*

Wizz: *I hadn't heard from Clive for ages and then I got a letter from him saying 'I've been living in Edinburgh in a flat with a guy called Robin Williamson. I hear you're working with Pete Stanley, why don't you come up and do a gig at my club and you can stay over at the place where I'm staying?'*

We arrived in the morning and went straight over to Mary Stewart's. It was difficult to find it first time because it was in the middle of a golf course, but we drove into this place which was like Alice's Restaurant, with kids and dogs running everywhere, and Clive came limping out to greet us.

The gig was amazing because they'd booked Davy Graham on the same bill. We arrived and there was Davy, dapper in a white suit with a blonde on his arm. The residents were the Incredibles, Hamish Imlach and Archie Fisher.

In the summer of 1964 Wizz also introduced Pete Stanley to Cornwall. Ralph McTell: *Wizz's beatnik reputation still followed him as the two*

49

trudged from pub to hotel to pub asking for playing work. In those days if a pub had any live music at all, it would be a rickety jazz duo or trio (fugitives from the waning Cornish Trad Jazz boom) or a bow-tied chappie plunking away on an electric organ!

So it was indeed a brave landlord, a Mr Green of The Mermaid in Porth, who gave the boys their first big break in Cornwall. Years later I learned that one of the things that inspired Ken Woollard to start the Cambridge Folk Festival was hearing Pete and Wizz at The Mermaid that first Summer.

Pete: *I remember busking in Newquay in 1964. We stayed in a tent on a campsite. The Mermaid gig was nice. Playing there became a regular thing, once or twice a week for at least two months.*

St Rumons Hotel in Newquay in the 50s. Another venue Pete and Wizz performed at the 1964.

Wizz: *Mick Softley came down in '64 and played with us in St Rumon's Hotel. Sandy and I, when we had our first kid, lived at Mick Softley's house for a few months one winter. Donovan used to sit in the audience when Mick used to play at The Cock in St Albans.*

On returning to London Wizz and Pete recorded a single and album with Columbia. The former was called 'The Ballad of Hollis Brown', and the latter '16 Tons of Bluegrass' (see photo in introduction). The recording sessions had been held in Regent Sound in Denmark Street: a popular, cheap studio also used by the Rolling Stones for their first

album. The cover shots for the album had been taken in Cornwall.
Wizz: *The photographs on 16 Tons are Holywell bay. And Sandy was in that picture but she was airbrushed out because she was in the background with the baby! The guy that took the photos in Newquay took the photos for the record. Ned (Ralph Clement) took lots of them. Ned also took the photo of me and Sandy by the Gannel.*

Attitudes towards the itinerant musicians were changing dramatically, and one person embodied the shift in their fortunes more than any other. His name was Donovan.

Chapter Four: Donovan and St Ives

Jonathon Xavier Coudrille moved to live in the seaside town of St Ives in West Cornwall as a young teenager at the beginning of the 60's: *St Ives then was full of very serious artists: Ben Nicholson, Barbara Hepworth and Patrick Heron were the holy trinity - then there was the gay scene at Trewyn House which was John Milne and his friends. A lot of very high profile actors and artists used to come down for their parties - quite a lot of faces from the 'Carry On' films used to turn up. One of my role models, Sven Berlin who was a great brawling and heterosexual artist, had just left St Ives and run off with poor old Victor Bramley's wife. But his shadow still hung over pubs like The Golden Lion where he would break noses and knock teeth out....*

The country-wide trad jazz revival of the early 60's had a strong support-base in Cornwall, as well as a ready supply of local brass-players. Jonathon: *There is a wonderful brass band tradition in Cornwall which most of the 'traddies' had been through. There was a band called the Atlantic All-Stars that did covers of Kenny Ball and others. I played piano as a teenager with Des Hockings' band. Des was a farmer's son from Zennor – a good trumpet player who went up to London and went pro with Monty Sunshine...*

Denys Val Baker was a freelance writer. As editor of the 'Cornish Review' and author of 'Britain's Art Colony by the Sea' he was at the time at the centre of Cornwall's cultural life, and close friend to artists like Sven Berlin. In the early 60's his eldest son Martin was another teenager passionate about jazz: *New Orleans revivalist jazz was all the rage in the circles we mixed in, and there was a great jazz club just outside St Ives at the Carbis Bay Memorial Hall which would be jam-packed every week with a regular local band playing. There were people from all over the country at the jazz club, you could tell where they came from by their dance styles, not only the town or city of origin but their actual individual jazz clubs.*

Depiction of the Val Baker house, St Christopher's, from 'The Door is Always Open' by Denys Val Baker. The property backed onto Porthmeor Beach and was home to six Val Baker children, The Mask Pottery, CND meetings and a café. Later, after the Val Bakers had left, it was the original location of Mask Folk Club.

Martin's love of jazz took him and his friends far afield: *In those days we would travel vast distances by thumb, hitch-hiking with just a small rucksack, a blanket and a tin mug - sleeping rough in the open air or at the homes of friends we met on the road. On a good day, and this was before the days of motorways, you could leave St Ives at 8 am and expect to be in Central London twelve hours later. In the early sixties we thumbed to jazz festivals in Manchester, Taunton, Bath, Bristol and in particular the annual bash at Richmond run by the National Jazz and Blues Federation.*

St Ives, just like Newquay, was experiencing an influx of unwelcome visitors. Martin: *St Ives then was a magnet for beatniks. Long-haired, bearded, clad in high desert boots and khaki clothes from the Army & Navy stores, they poured into the town from all over the place. They lived in encampments on the hills outside St Ives and spent the daytime lounging around the town strumming guitars and smoking dope. Rod Stewart, Donovan, Julie Driscoll and John Lennon were rumoured to have been amongst them.*

To us teenagers, they were romantic figures. They came from London and the northern industrial cities, a much more classless subculture than the hippies of the later sixties who were much more likely to be the children of the middle classes. MVB memoirs

Jonathon: *Beatniks came to St Ives in quantity and were hugely unpopular with the town elders but immensely attractive to youngsters like myself. It was an intellectual movement. They used to sit around reading: can you believe that! A lot of them came down with guitars and banjos on their back and some of them could play them very well. They all read Kerouac's 'On the Road', they were all acquainted with Woody Guthrie and there was a strong visible left-wing bias. Beatniks were political, they were intellectual, they were sexy, they were cool. We all aspired to beatnik chic...that was the style of the day...*

In 1961 the town's elders' battles with the beatniks made national news, just as it had in Newquay. John the Fish: *The Sloop in St Ives banned anyone with a beard and Giles published a great cartoon. There were songs written about it and it became national news, just like Newquay.*

The cartoon appeared in The Daily Express on Tuesday 11th April 1961. Toni Carver, editor of the St Ives Times and Echo: *The beatnik era kicked off big time with 'St Ives and the Beatniks: Giles gives the bare facts'. It picked up on this story that St Ives licensees had banned beatniks from the town's pubs. We published the cartoon in the St Ives Times and Echo the following Friday.*

The local paper suggested that resident artists and beatniks were indistinguishable, and a letter from artist Anthony Shiels, who became known later for photographing the Loch Ness monster, confirmed this: he too had suffered the indignity of being refused service.

Then the following week The Times and Echo ran the headline: *'Public urged to help repel Beatniks'*. The council was encouraging local people to cooperate in *'ridding our town of the blight of this modern day tramp'*.

St. Ives and the Beatniks : Giles gives the bare facts

ARTISTS IN DUFFLE-COATS & DRAINPIPES WILL NOT BE SERVED

NO BEATNIKS SERVED

ONLY GENUINE ARTISTS SERVED

CLEAR THE BEATNIKS OUT OF CORNWALL S.T IVES LANDLORDS SAY BAN ARTISTS IN FANCY-DRES & LONG-HAIRED INTERLECTULS PROTECT THE REGULARS

" I assure you, sir, that I am a very genuine artist."

The Daily Express April 11th 1961: Beatniks in St Ives were as unwelcome as they were in Newquay, and they were attracting just as much newsprint, if not more.

Toni: *I was a young teenager in St Ives (14). We would get flak from the parents saying 'stay away from these horrible hairy people, don't go near them they're disgusting'... One of my first jobs was delivering signs to the pubs. They read: 'The management reserves the right to refuse to serve beatniks'. Sid Woosley, landlord of The Union was ex-military, and survivor of the Japanese prison camps so he had a very, very grim view of anybody with long hair...*

The Daily Express was only one of a number of 'nationals' to take an interest in the beatnik story. The Guardian, for example, ran several articles and suggested that St Ives was the ultimate beatnik destination: *'For those that have been tramping it for several years the beat starts in London where most disillusion is born, proceeds to Newcastle, Birmingham and Bristol and then on to Brixham and finally St Ives, still the centre of beatnik life...St Ives is most appealing in the summer months when there are the scrapings of an existence from the holiday trade...but at this time of year a visit to the labour exchange to collect the weekly dole is the safest means of enduring life until the warmer weather*....Guardian 1964

Ian Anderson is editor of fRoots, based in Bristol: *I'm still stupidly proud of having been refused service in The Sloop in '64. And me a mere weekend-beatnik! It was a rite of folk/blues passage in Weston-super-Mare to pile into a car full of guitars and banjos and head for Cornwall.*

Ralph McTell: *To be honest when we first arrived, you can understand why they were so suspicious of us beatniks. Cornwall was a very naive and uncorrupted place. It was gentler and more relaxed: a mixture of the parochial and mystical. It was like another country.*

Toni: *After the newspaper coverage St Ives eclipsed Newquay as the home of the British beatniks, which is what attracted Donovan and Dave Mills to the town in 1963. Beatniks and then hippies were a major feature of St Ives until 1973 when the last group was evicted from Steeple Woods by the council.*

Later in the 60's Donovan Leitch would have eight top ten hit records. In 1961 at the age of 15, however, he was still a 'mod', living in Hatfield near St Albans, and travelling with other mods on scooters to watch bands like The High Numbers (later The Who). By 1962 Donovan had found himself at a local art college and reinvented himself as a beatnik. Donovan: *That Summer found me lying on the grass with long-haired girls in 'sloppy Joes', sandals and black mascara, talking painting, pottery and poetry, and debating revolution and banning The Bomb. We loved the songs of Joan Baez, Pete Seeger and the incomparable Woody Guthrie.* HGM

Inspired, again, by the twin figures of Kerouac and Guthrie, the young Donovan had a yearning for travel and for freedom. It was a feeling he shared with his friend Gypsy Dave Mills. Donovan: *Gypsy Dave would - in the coming months - help me break free of my small-town world...We shared a dream and a desire for freedom and the open road...summer was a-coming in and young beats were feeling the call of the seaside. As the author Colin Wilson said in his book of the same name 'the outsider finds his life all unreal, a fake performance by*

Gypsy Dave carries Donovan's guitar as they are seen arriving in St Ives in 'A Boy Called Donovan'.

everyone around him. Only one thing can break the feeling of alienation – to leave'.

Donovan hitched to Cornwall via Devon with his friend in the spring of 1963. Donovan: *It was word of mouth around St. Albans that all the students would go down in the summers to St Ives, which of course has been an artist destination and community for over a hundred years. There is even a Leach Pottery there, though it has a different spelling from my own last name (Leitch). So off we went, Gypsy Dave and I, to join thousands of other young Beats that summer…*

Gypsy Dave: *Hitchhiking was fairly easy in those days. It was the main means of transport used by our Forces when they had any sort of home leave. Often the first thing we were asked when entering a car, was what service we were from - usually in a voice that held amazement at how low that service must have fallen to include lads of our decrepitude! We'd heard about the artistic 'bohemian' circle that was living in St Ives and wanted to experience some of that lifestyle. The fact that a lot of art school girls found their way down there in the summer holidays was a plus for us young lads too…*

Ferrell's in 2004, one of the few bakeries remaining from the 60's. It supplied Donovan with Saffron buns, so inspiring the song 'Mellow Yellow'.

Donovan immediately felt at home: *'I am at last in the bohemian world where I belong', I thought. The holiday season had not yet begun and we were the first beatniks to arrive in St Ives that year.*

As art students both were aware of St Ives' importance in the artworld. The doyenne of international modern sculpture who was living in the centre of the town, Barbara Hepworth, had recently completed a large sculpture for a flagship John Lewis store in Oxford Street. Gypsy Dave does not remember meeting many artists in St Ives, however: *We did get to meet a couple of the famous potters there and saw their work. I believe the visual artists were a bit cliquey. Don't forget we were barely 16 at that time. I was still 15 when I first arrived with Don and I think he was only just 16. (on May 10th)*

One of the potters Don and Gypsy met was Jess Val Baker, of the Mask Pottery. Wife of Denys, they met her through Jane, her daughter. Jane: *We became good friends during that period. We spent a lot of time on the harbour wall just looking at people, or we sat on the beach and talked about what was going on in our generation...*

58

Don got a job washing dishes at the beach café. I think Don came two years running...his first girlfriend worked at the Porthminster Hotel...He was an introverted, quiet person. Gypsy Dave was his spokesman and seemed to do everything for him. Gypsy was like his minder and they were very good friends. They were very close. I've got a lovely photo of them taken by the harbour when they decided to go - its Gypsy Dave and Donovan waving back...

Donovan describes thinking of the seagulls of St Ives as 'handsome scavengers': *I noticed that the Ships Chandler sold the caps worn by the Breton fishermen who docked in St Ives, and I decided I would be a handsome scavenger too.* The cap he bought in St Ives, he wore when he made his first television appearances 18 months later. Together with the harmonica, it immediately led him to be compared to Bob Dylan, though in fact both men had independently modelled themselves on Woody Guthrie.

He and Gypsy Dave survived initially by begging and petty thieving. Donovan: *We would stroll around to the small bakery which sold the sweet bread called saffron cake, a yellow loaf packed with raisins. The nice lady would give us yesterday's loaves for nothing. We washed it down with stolen milk.*

Conceived and made in St Ives, Barbara Hepworth's Winged Figure' was installed in Oxford Street in May 1963 – the month that Donovan arrived in Cornwall. Photo: St Ives Times and Echo.

They would sleep on the beach, when not moved on by the town's late-night policeman, or in the woods below the Tregenna Castle Hotel where they used a hut constructed out of stout branches intertwined with smaller ones. Gypsy Dave: *A little more daring than most - or a little madder - we threw ourselves into living. We lived in beach huts, pillboxes, tents, the occasional paid room, a hut on Crab Rock and out on the open sands of a moon and star encrusted beach. Also for a short time, in a cramped dwelling made of branches and plastic bags that a friend and I had made in the woods of the grounds of a swanky hotel. I never had money in my pocket. Never knew where my next meal would come from or how I would get it. Things turned up or they didn't.*

Their sleep was aided by cannabis. Donovan: *We showed some caution in those days but not much as smoking hash was only done by the beats, and the police were not yet on the lookout for it. Occasionally we even smoked joints in cinemas. Beats were a minority then, drop outs from art schools, campers, trad-jazz enthusiasts, blues singers, folk musicians who listened to obscure jazz records, blind singers and jug-bands. Everyone took pills of many sorts and talked their tongues as dry as old leather into the night, and sometimes even past the dawn. Apart from the lack of food, all the kids were healthy then, sleeping out under the stars...*

Later in the Summer Donovan took a job washing dishes at The Harbour Bar, where there was a jukebox that would play the first Beatles singles. His wage allowed him to rent a room near Porthmeor Studios on the beach adjacent to what is now Tate St Ives which he and a friend, Derek, named Studio 2000. Their 'pad' became a regular venue for parties.

On one occasion the police called round having been tipped off by some anxious parents. Donovan: *the party was in full swing, the beer flowing, guitars bashing, pill-heads freaking but the real cool beats were making a whole scene, lying in a corner rolling and smoking, rolling and smoking. The inspector excused himself for interrupting and read from a list of runaways. Of course if the runaways were there, no one would let on'.*

Donovan yawning in the hut on Crab Rock in St Ives. Sitting opposite is American Derroll Adams (from A boy called Donovan 1966). The hut is one of two that overlook Porthminster Beach.

The new-found money was also invested in a guitar. It was Donovan's first, bought from a fellow beat called John Vanstone for £3.10s. Donovan: *John Vanstone was a character!*

Whilst in St Ives Donovan learnt to play 'Working on the Railroad', 'Careless Love' and 'Cocaine Blues'. Soon the guitar was beginning to pay for itself. Gypsy Dave: *Donovan had been practicing any song he could lay his ears on and we two were beginning to go out on the streets - Dono with his guitar and me with a paper and comb or a kazoo. I played the fool a lot when passing the hat round and that helped a lot. It was handy if we were stony broke.*

I thought we were lucky that the audience paid good money just to hear Donovan sing - we had no idea then that the reason was some strange magic Donovan possessed. A spellbinding ingredient that was to turn him into a millionaire and one of the best known and influential artists of the mid-sixties.

Donovan singing 'Catch the Wind' - his first top ten hit - on Porthminster beach in St Ives. Cornish music promoter Martin Val Baker is on the right of the photograph, with sister Jane more central.

Gypsy Dave: *St. Ives was an experience never to be forgotten - It held so many 'firsts' for me. It was where I first fell deeply in love; first felt the knowledge of brotherhood; first realized that you aren't going to die before you're supposed to; first understood the true meaning of 'freedom of spirit'. First knew for sure, that each man is his own island; first welcomed the fact that God was in no man's church, but lived in the very core of our own being; first got drunk on something other than alcohol. First became aware that colleges didn't hold a monopoly on intelligence; first understood that sex is a responsibility as well as a fantastic pleasure; first realized that governments don't really govern, they only make a show of it...*

Donovan returned briefly to St Ives in 1964, but he spent most of the summer that year in Torquay, in Devon. He started writing his own songs, and made a demo tape that eventually reached the producer of a new youth TV programme 'Ready Steady Go'. Wearing the cap he had originally bought in Cornwall, he appeared on the programme in January 1965: *I now wore the cap partly as a homage to Woody Guthrie and copied too the phrase he had on his guitar: 'This machine kills fascists' - except I dropped the last word, thinking fascism was already dead. My machine would kill greed and delusion.*

In March his first single 'Catch the Wind' entered the charts at number 4. *After five 'Ready Steady Go' programmes...my name, my face and my music were now in every home in Britain. I was happening on a major scale.*

Donovan's meteoric rise to fame in the UK, was remarkably, then repeated in the US, where 'Catch the Wind' went to reach number 3 in the Billboard 100.

Meanwhile the presence of beatniks in St Ives throughout the sixties, continued to be seen as a problem, and the council went to new extremes to contain it. In October 1963, around the time that Donovan and his friends were leaving the town, it was announced that the 'beatnik wall' on the harbour front would be made more 'uncomfortable'.

Jonathon Coudrille: *There used to be a great big thick concrete block wall in front of The Sloop. It had been put there to keep the German tanks out during the war. It was a meeting place. A wonderful thing to sit on, and if you were tired you could lie on it. All the corduroyed denim-clad beatniks used to hitchhike down and flake out on the wall. But the council decided to ridge the wall so that they could no longer do so.*

Jane Val Baker: *We all congregated there. Anybody that was working would bring food for the others. It was great: there was a great sense of community amongst the beats. I stole food from home to feed my mates there, even though my parents were poor.*

Jane got to know many of the older beatniks after attending CND marches with them in the late 50's: *We went on all the CND marches together with my brothers and sisters and mother and father - they were very active.*

Martin Val Baker: *There were frequent meetings of the local Campaign for Nuclear Disarmament at my father's home, St Christopher's. In 1961 forty-one of us boarded the coach at Camborne and when it returned from London the following day there were only eleven on it - the rest of us had been gaoled. This was the occasion of the*

Beat 'sympathisers' stage a play by John Antrobus in November 1963 on the beatnik wall. A St Ives resident, Antrobus was co-author with Spike Milligan of 'The Bed-Sitting Room'. Photo: Times and Echo

demonstration when over 1,200 were arrested as anti-nuclear protesters blocked Trafalgar Square.

In November 1963 a different kind of protest, which included especially written music by Jane's father, was orchestrated by John Antrobus, St Ives resident and writing partner of Spike Milligan. It centred on The Beatnik Wall, and Jonathon Coudrille also contributed: *It was fairly puerile satirical street theatre and poetry:*
We sat on this wall many summers ordinary folk you and I,
It offers a seat for all-comers concrete hygienic and dry.
Committees who sit on their chairs nice and plastic,
agree that the wall should be pointed and that
any beatnik they find with a concave behind,
shall be run out of town by and by.

Puerile it may have been, but it still made BBC's 'Tonight' on national prime-time TV, and indirectly led to one of Cornwall's first folk clubs. Jonathon: *The protest led to me writing political satire for the Today Radio 4 programme and I ended up performing for Westward TV. At Westward I met Cyril Tawney who later became like an Uncle to me.*

Meeting the Plymouth-based song-writer inspired Jonathon to open The Mermaid folk club in St Ives: Jonathon: *My father had bought the old*

64

lemonade factory at the end of Fish Street. He called it 'Mermaid Arts Centre' and my mother and I ran a folk club there. The space was a gallery during the day, with father's studio upstairs. I was 17 at the time. It would have been '63. It probably was the first Folk Club in Cornwall.

Jane Val Baker: *The Mermaid Folk club was great! Dark with lots of people - it was fabulous. I remember John the Fish and Pete Chatterton singing at the Mermaid. Pete was a real star. Many beautiful girls with guitars wandered through all the time. People mainly aged from 16 to 30 were in there. And all the young artists would have gone.*

Jonathan: *Everybody sat on the concrete floor which was wonderful because from the stage you could see up the girl's skirts! Lots of the beatniks came to The Mermaid. They paid a small entrance fee and we sold soft drinks. I used to take Hudson (the car) to Jolly's at Hayle to get their substitute Coca Cola and appalling orange squash and so forth.*

We were packed every time we ran, which was two nights a week in the season. My father enjoyed the company of Pete Chatterton. He was a Yorkshire boy who was one of the finger-in-the-ear brigade of singers. Very powerful, wonderful voice, but got himself put in jail I think for a drugs offence.

The Young Tradition also came down. I met Pete Bellamy through singer Vernon Rose. Pete was lovely and he lived at the house with us for a couple of years. Then when he told me that he'd formed The Young Tradition with Heather and Royston they became the house band for a season and they lived at the house.

I would have sung comic material of my own, long on lyrical cleverness, but short on folk authenticity and gravitas. I did however have the requisite beard and home-made plaid shirt! An evening may well have closed with everyone joining in with 'Wild Mountain Thyme'.

Friday, April 24, 1964   PRICE 3d.

'Beatnik wall'— with knobs on

Workmen with pneumatic drills have been engaged this week on what the Borough Council hope will be the final chapter of the highly controversial story of St. Ives "beatnik wall." The wall, which faces the Sloop Inn and is nearly 40 yards long and over two feet wide, has been reduced from chest-height to less than knee-height. A series of metal stumps is to be drilled into it which will permit sitting, but discourage lying, on the remains of the wall. Last summer, largely as a result of complaints that groups of beatniks congregating near the wall and lying on it were giving the town a bad name and driving away trade, the Council's Harbour and Beaches Committee held a special meeting and drew up a plan for discouraging "undesirable elements." They recommended that the wall, built as a war-time defence measure, should be surmounted by a ridge to make lying on it difficult and uncomfortable. The Council agreed, but after protests outside and inside the Council chamber, the scheme was held-up while other suggestions were advanced and considered, including the complete removal of the wall.

In April 1964 The Beatnik Wall was removed: 'Last summer largely as a result of complaints that groups of beatniks congregating near the wall and lying on it were giving the town a bad name and driving away trade the Council…drew up a plan for discouraging 'undesirable elements''

I went onto the circuit myself. I played at the Folk Cottage, and Bungies and Les Cousins. I met Ralph McTell and Wizz in London. Later, strangely, The Mermaid Inn in Porth, where they played, bought my father's painting of a mermaid that had been one of the features of our own club in St Ives.

After more protracted debates The Beatnik Wall was finally removed completely in the spring of 1964. Undeterred, beatniks continued to visit St Ives, and continued to make national press: *From the size of this year's invasions of resorts, mainly in the west, many feel that the beatnik numbers are growing. Beatniks themselves, jealous of their minority, estimate their full-time strength at several hundred, perhaps a thousand…the beatniks have deliberately opted out of society and its responsibilities…* Observer, October 4th, 1964

This was especially so in the summer of 1969 when there were two significant flashpoints: '*St Ives beatniks beaten in the battle of the clifftop*': *Fifty beatniks who had occupied an old cliff lookout hut were evicted by 14 council workmen...'We are kids who have dropped out of the working class rat-race or the bourgeois ghetto to which it leads and have gone on the roads...if we are being persecuted its because our existence gives the lie to the phoney securities of modern society...*' The Guardian, July 5th 1969

'*This was a week in which 300 local people surrounded a house where 21 beatniks were blockaded, literally screaming with hatred*'
The Guardian, July 12th 1969

'*A petition signed by 2,321 residents and holidaymakers at St Ives, Cornwall was handed to the Mayor, Ald. Archie Knight during the weekend. It calls for tighter vagrancy laws to rid the town of beatniks.*'
Daily Telegraph, 21 July 1969

Chapter 5: The Count House and Brenda Wootton

Folk music at the beginning of the 60's had been played informally by teenagers on the beaches, but it did not yet have established audiences, venues or promoters in Cornwall. Lots of the local teenage skiffle musicians like Truro-based Roger Taylor (who went on to form 'Queen'), bought electric instruments, and found an audience playing rock 'n' roll or 'beat music' instead.

The Staggerlees were the most popular Rock n Roll or Beat group to play in St Ives in the early 60's, where they vied for an audience with local jazz and dance bands. Two members of The Staggerlees later became music promoters in Cornwall. Dave Penprase opened folk venue Room at the Top, and Pete Bawden PJ's where Queen, and pre-Queen group Smile played on over 10 occasions.

Pete Berryman, later a key member of the folk scene, was one of them. He was born and brought up in the resort of Newquay: *I was aware of skiffle but it was Elvis posturing with his guitar that inspired me to play. After school I joined a band called The Drifters. They were copying Cliff Richard and the Shadows and they had the all the steps...There was loads of work for the groups in Cornwall then because we'd taken the work away from the dance bands, which is a shame because they were really good musicians.*

Pete Berryman's school band: The Launceston Jazz Quartet

In the early 1960's John Langford, or John the Fish, moved from London to Penzance in West Cornwall. He started working as a fisherman, but still played his guitar and became a cornerstone of the emerging Cornish folk scene: *Our attempts at fishing kept Newlyn amused for months! But I found that playing the guitar and singing opened doors for me, and got me invited to all the parties...*

Mike Sagar, like John the Fish, would later become one of Brenda Wootton's accompanists. Mike: *John was spectacularly unsuccessful as a fisherman. These guys came down from London and bought a boat. The first time they went out in it they tied it to the quay and went to the pub. When they came back they found it literally hanging from the quay because the tide had gone out!*

Mike was a teenager, a few years younger than Fish. As he explains, beat culture was finding its expression amongst resident Cornish youngsters elsewhere in Penwith: *I was part of a subculture that was into long jumpers, espresso coffees, joss sticks and jazz. West Cornwall was like a little arty outpost on its own, with strong connections to London rather than anywhere else.*

John the Fish crouches with crew mates on The Falcon

Cornish beats were in the process of switching their musical allegiances from jazz to folk: *Nothing really happened in West Cornwall folk-wise until 62-63. Then our own folk culture came back to us via America - via the first Joan Baez records. Before that there were bands like The Weavers who did things like 'On Top of Old Smokey' but they were n't cool if you were into beat culture and jazz. But when the Baez stuff came over it came part of the protest movement, with Dylan and people like that writing their own songs in the folk style.*

Dylan's first album was largely a collection of traditional songs, but it was with 'The Freewheelin' Bob Dylan' of 1963 that he established his credentials as the outstanding American song-writer of his generation. It was a decisive moment and even teenage jazz aficionado from St Ives, Martin Val Baker, found himself switching to folk: *The records of Joan Baez and Bob Dylan lead my generation to folk music. Most of us agreed that Joan Baez and particularly Bob Dylan were gods.*

The latter's 'Masters of War' confirmed me as a pacifist, and 'God on Our Side' as an atheist.

A couple of informal folk clubs opened up in West Cornwall in about 1963, possibly slightly preceding The Mermaid in St Ives, and reflecting a trend that was beginning to affect the whole country. John

70

the Fish recalls: *There was a cafe at the top of Morrab Road in Penzance run by Harry Graves. The Morrab café. As more and more youngsters went there, he opened up the cellar and called it 'The Graveyard'. In fact Harry took a shine to me and my friend Ian and when we ordered our meals he would shout down to the kitchen 'Two meals for the fishermen'. In no time at all it was abbreviated to John the Fish.*

'How to Spot a Beatnik' was published in St Ives in about 1963 by Ian Todd. It featured cartoons by local artist, Cedric Rogers which included images of beatniks on 'The Beatnik Wall' reproduced in The Guardian in 1966. Photo Toni Carver

The Layabouts were Penzance's premier rock 'n' roll band. *The pub in Chapel Street - The Turk's Head - was another place where on a Sunday night we would get together and have a session. Tim Knight of The Layabouts and Mike Sagar would drop in and play.*

Mike got to know Fish at one of the local club-nights. Mike: *The first folk thing I remember happening was Saturday night sessions at the Turk's Head. There was a local guy called Philip Rowley who'd learnt 'Lamorna' off the Matthews Brothers in Porthgwara, (featured in Peter Kennedy's recordings of 1956) so we would play that. Then John the Fish turned up. He was a deeply beatnicky person. He was a loner - living in squats - and very alternative. Bloody great beard, he wore big coats, sat in a corner on his own singing all these songs, and we learnt them all off him. He was a huge influence on me.*

Fish: *The Layabouts introduced me to Tel Mann who was a country & western singer with a big voice who used to yodel, and we started working together as John and Tell, when we were approached by J Ian Todd and John Wood. They'd just bought the Count House at Botallack and they had a couple of fellers they knew called Mel and Miles who were going to do cabaret there. They were both school teachers, but Ian and John couldn't wait until the holidays so they approached Tel and I and offered to pay us a pound a night.*

Toni Carver: *Ian Todd first came to St Ives circa 1958 or '59. For a while he ran a printing business famously publishing Cedric Rogers' 'How to Spot a Beatnik'(see picture).*

The Count House at Botallack was situated high on perilous cliffs, its windows looking across the Atlantic Ocean towards America. Idyllic in the summer, in the winter it was pounded by the elements. Nearby were derelict mine-workings that had inspired a journalist writing in The Guardian (1964) to compare the landscape to Tolkein's Mordor.

Judi Rea was married to Ian Todd: *When we moved to Botallack it was very basic. There was just one cold tap. Ian and I lived in the top half and the Woods lived in the bottom half. There was a barn there that was empty, and, as we couldn't afford to go out for entertainment, Ian and John thought 'Let's bring the entertainment to us'.*

Tel Mann and John The Fish: Photo Anthony Barraclough

Mel and Miles: Photo Anthony Barraclough

The seats were benches from old Methodist chapels. And we put fishing nets up to stop the ceiling falling down on people! The walls were painted with lime I think. The toilets were Elsans - chemical toilets - that the boys used to empty in the interval down the nearest mine-shaft, until the council got a bit stroppy. It got so big they had to get proper toilets fitted eventually.

Everything was done on the cheap because we were very broke. Both families were. The Count House did make some money, but the boys would have to do other bits of work - including daffodil-picking. At one time Shirley and I used to make fisherman's caps and smocks which the boys sold in St Ives. It was very much hand-to-mouth living at the time, but it was good fun and of course it was in the most beautiful place.

The Count House started out as homemade music, then grew like topsy. The first performers were a guy they had heard playing jugs on the beach, and someone from St Just council who came and played spoons!

John the Fish and Tel were the first of the more professional performers at the Count House when it opened in time for the summer (1964). Fish: *We would sit around for the best part of the evening and no-one would turn up! Perhaps a family would turn up, or maybe two if we were lucky and we would sit there and chat to them and sing a few songs. But soon it got really popular, and when Mel and Miles did come down Ian said 'sorry but it's a fully fledged folk club - no cabaret - you'd better go and learn some folk songs'. So they went down to the library...*

There was a considerable groundswell of interest in folk music by 1964. Mike Sagar: *When John (the Fish) was pulled out there, we all literally followed. This folky thing that was happening in Penzance just migrated, so they had a ready-made audience which they weren't prepared for. We thought it was all great fun to scrounge rides or catch buses or hitchhike to this god-forsaken place on the cliffs, and stay there for as late as possible! And all the girls would have to convince their parents that all they were doing were singing folk songs and drinking coffee, which was absolutely true.*

And a lot of the parents then came along to check it out and stayed, as they found they were included. So it went from being a few clued- up people to a very multi-gendered and -aged democratic institution because everybody enjoyed it equally.

74

John Sleep was another of the performers at the Count House during its first year of operation. He had moved near to Newquay: *Living in Crantock, I met a chap called John Hayday and we both did a bit of singing in the hotels. I was teaching, but my salary was only £600 a year so we had to do something to earn a bit more money. My set was more traditional folk - some sea shanties, and Cyril Tawney who had some good songs: Baby Lie Easy, The Oggy Man and Diesel and Shale.*

Mike Sagar: *I remember that first Christmas at the Count House we all clubbed together and bought John (The Fish) a coat. He was so grateful, he was so sweet. He's a lovely guy. I love John, lots of us did, and do.*

In 1965, as the club was entering its second year, Des Hannigan was living Glasgow. He and a friend had planned to go busking in Europe but ended up diverting to St Ives instead: *We went to The Mermaid club run by Jonathan Coudrille. He invited us up to sing but was outraged when we asked for some money after the performance! Then he said 'if you want to be paid try this place on the cliffs at Botallack'.*

Tel Man : Photo Anthony Barraclough

75

Des recalls his first visit: *I was really tickled. I remember I was very impressed by the setting. It was amazing there. The mining landscape was desolate in many ways but also eerily romantic. It genuinely felt like the end of the world.*

I walked in the door and there were John the Fish and Terry with their beards. It was quite funny. Terry looked like a jolly little guy and John was an absolute picture and they were singing American folk songs. I could sing unaccompanied and that had huge appeal then. If you could stick your finger in your ear and sing reasonably authentically then you were assumed to be the real thing.

Ian heard that I was a Scottish singer and said 'can you sing a couple of numbers?' So I did two or three and he gave me 10 shillings which I thought remarkable.

All those involved with The Count House remember Brenda Wootton, who became the first lady of Cornish folk, visiting it initially as a member of the audience. When interviewed in the 80's she said: *Susan, my daughter, who was then about 14 wanted to go with her friends. I said 'What? Go where? An old barn on the cliffs listening to folk music?' Being the sort of parents we were we felt it had to be vetted. All sorts of things could have been going on up there! So Susan wasn't allowed to go, but my husband and I decided to go. And there they all were sitting drinking coffee, and there was a whole world of music, some familiar like some country-style songs.* FCHTC

Brenda was quite strict, and, a generation older, initially wary of the beatnik sub-culture. Sue*: Probably around 1964 myself and a friend used to catch the bus to St Ives - where I was NOT allowed to go, because of the beatniks. We used to sit in the Sugar & Spice cafe near the bus station, just to sit and look at them, but once I got found out and the resulting punishment left a lasting impression on me!*

However, Brenda was quickly won round by The Count House. Brenda: *Various people went with their children. You couldn't catch a bus there so you needed Mum and Dad to get you there so the Mum and Dads was sitting in one part and the youngsters in another part. And of course when I look back it was so innocent and so lovely. In the summer time you'd arrive and as you were going in you'd take a look across to the mine stacks, or down at the sea, or over to the Scillies, and the sun*

76

would set red on your face. Other times you couldn't see for the mist and the fog, and in the winter it used to be that cold we'd take a cardboard box to put our feet in! FCHTC

It was later that year that Brenda started performing at the club. John Sleep: *I remember her as a person in the audience who would join in. She was a menace!*

Des: *Being Brenda, bless her, she would sit about five rows down, where she was a focal point, and she would hum along very loudly. There was always that audience participation element but she would sing along when no-one else was!*

John the Fish: *When Brenda started to come along we would hear this amazing harmony coming from the audience, and thought: who's this singing? Eventually we pinned it down to Brenda. Of course we tried to lure her up onto the stage 'you've got to come up and sing' and that was the start of her folk career.*

Ian Todd serving coffee at The Count House. Headline 'The Lure of Cornwall's Folk Trend' West Briton August 18th 1966. Bottles of Coke and the LP 'More singing at the Count House' are also for sale.

Brenda Wootton's repertoire was initially limited to the songs she had learnt growing up in Newlyn near Penzance. Brenda: *Ian Todd kept pushing me. Are you going to sing tonight? Are you going to sing? So one night I stood up, and I didn't know folk songs but I sang a song that I knew, and that was 'Lamorna'. And that was it. Ian asked if I would sing regular there.*

Brenda Wootton (nee Ellery) had attended the Girl's Grammar School in Penzance, and though she didn't learn to play an instrument, between the ages of about 8 and 14 she sang in the local Methodist Chapel choir. Daughter Sue takes up the story: *After mother left school she worked in the telephone exchange in Penzance. She would organise dances and events like staff outings. My father met my mother at one of these dances, and they got married in about 47-48.*

The newly-weds lived in a few different houses in and around Sennen near Lands End. Sue: *Through all this mother was just a housewife, trying to make ends meet, and they were quite poor. She used to go out carol-singing with the locals. Their carol-singing treks would take them all over Sennen for miles. They would go to each individual farm, walking across the cliffs carrying home-made lanterns. I can remember the lanterns that father used to make: little tin cans with holes cut in them on sticks.*

Round about that time Brenda set up Sennen drama group and every year they would put on a pantomime. They could n't afford to buy scripts or anything, so she would write them herself.

Mike Sagar met Brenda through his involvement in local drama. Mike: *I was involved in all her pantomimes. She started doing them in Sennen. Then we would tour them around the church halls in West Cornwall, with varying results as you can imagine. Some of them were very primitive. Some of the audience were very primitive!*

With titles such as 'Grizzley Beard', 'The shoes that were danced to pieces', 'Abu Hassan' and 'The Stones of Le Menec' the pantomimes which ran for several years were often based on folk tales. Sue: *There's a Breton legend that once every hundred years the stones of Le Menec would come down to the river to drink, and when they did the holes they left would be filled with treasure.*

An early photo of Fish and Brenda on stage at the Count House.

We moved to Penzance in 1959. They bought a house in Leskinnick Street near the station, and for a few years we did B & B and I used to help with breakfast even if I was going to school. I think father worked for Rediffusion doing TV and radio repair. Wherever we lived he had sheds absolutely filled to the gunwales with TV radio parts which used to drive mother mad...

Brenda's brother, Peter, went to Bath College of Art at Corsham. In 1963 he decided he wanted to come back to Cornwall and set up his own pottery and Brenda ended up working there, at Tremaen Pottery as a potter between 1963 and 1974.

Once Brenda had become a regular performer at the Count House, John the Fish ended up as her accompanist. Fish: *I just fell in to it. I was the one that was there. At the time there was Des, Handshake, and me. I was there nearly every night - I needed the money, I'd given up the fishing. Plus it was an ambition that I'd had for years and years. It was something I really wanted: singing and entertaining people.*

Fish describes his working relationship with Brenda: *We would look around for songs. We would share songs. I had a wealth of songs and song books, and she would learn things from other people when they came down. Brenda's interest in Cornish folk came later. We were still mainly doing bits of jazz and blues, and English and American folk.*

Sue: *Brenda started singing every week, with Fish. He would have come round to our house to practice. And really she had no repertoire to start with. Sometimes she would pick up an old spiritual that she knew, or a song that she'd heard somewhere. Brenda liked blues, but, unlike Fish, she had n't been exposed to that much of it. I suppose there was less of it around in Cornwall, but we were unusual because we had a television in the 50's. A tiny little box television, so we must have picked up some music on there.*

Tablelamps made in the heyday of the Tremaen Pottery.

Steve Hall, Brenda and Fish at Botallack. Photo Sue Ellery.

Two recordings were made and released as records, the first on 31.10.64 the second a year later on 11.11.65.

As Ian Todd recalled in the 80's: *People were saying 'we've got nothing to remember our summer holiday down here' so we did an EP in the October. I persuaded Mel and Miles to come back down for the recording...I couldn't afford to finance a record so we sold shares and people bought shares in the record, got the free record and some money back. We had a fantastic response. We pressed 500, had it recorded and got the label produced and we sold all 500 in 6 weeks - by Christmas. So the following year we made an LP.* FCHTC

John The Fish *The first record predated Brenda and Des. It was an EP called 'Singing at the Count House'. Then they brought out 'More singing at the Count House'*

The dog Kega in the photo belonged to Ian Todd. He used to warn people 'look out for her because when you start your car she will go for your exhaust pipe'. One day she went for the exhaust pipe of Ian's own car when he stuck it in reverse, and he - sadly - ran her over. The photo was taken only a few hundred yards from the Count House. The tin mine on the cliff looks like it would be The Crowns.

Photo from the front cover of 'More Singing at The Count House'. L to R: Brenda, Fish (standing), Mel and Miles, Des Hannigan (standing).

Below the photograph on the sleeve of 'More Singing...' are excerpts from The Guardian's 1964 article about the club. Other reporters are known to have visited. Fish: *Angela Rippon was sent down to do an interview when it first opened. She was working for Westward TV in Plymouth.*

The photos on the back of the LP are a reminder that the audience was quite youthful. Des: *There was a huge local following. They were mainly local youngsters: many arty, creative types in their last years at school or starting at college. Those nets in the photos were everywhere you looked: in cafés in Penzance and restaurants in St Ives. Pilchard driving, where they caught pilchards using very fine black nets with cork floats, had effectively died out and there was a vast amount of old nets and glass buoys lying about.*

Fish: *The Count House was an idyllic set up. A beautiful place to be, though not the easiest place to find. Ian advertised for people to do a residency there, which meant they would sing every night of the week but have the day off to do whatever they wanted to. People flocked to come. Alex Atterson, Gerry Lockran, Alex Campbell, Bill Clifton, Todd Lloyd, The Haverim. No end of people came down. I was a resident for most of the time it was open. Tel got a bit uncomfortable with the fact I was spending more time there accompanying Brenda, so he opened his own club in Penzance called Tell-a-Tale in Chapel Street.*

Photo from the back cover of 'More Singing at The Count House'

Des: *Gerry Lockran (Loughran) was the first booked professional singer and he was terrific. Ian would have organised it. Gerry stayed in my cottage in Penzance. Lovely man. He died quite young but he was a terrific blues singer.*

Sue: *I remember having a crush on Gerry Lockran. Mind you so did Gerry Lockran. He was adorable because he was so full himself. He thought he was the bee's knees and God's gift. I also remember Cliff Aungier, Wizz, and Diz Disley.*

More amateur musicians could turn up unannounced and perform as 'itinerants'. Des: *We did n't audition them beforehand. We just threw them on. Ian and I worked out this system where we'd give them one song, and if they were good we'd ask for another.*

Judi: *We had all night sessions which were amazing. People would come down from Birmingham and from right up north for the whole weekend just for the experience. They would travel down during the day - stay for the night session - then go back the next day.*

We were not licensed so people just brought their own beer. But we sold pasties. We'd bring them in from Warren's in St Just and heat them up in the stove in the house, then Shirley, John Wood's wife, and I would rush them out at half-time.

Brenda: *The all-night sessions were funny. You were determined to stay there till the morning. Or Susan was. And me being her Mum stayed with her.*

Mike Sagar: *I just remember the audience itself which was like an amazing choir - they picked up all the songs and sang along with tremendous gusto.*

Brenda Wootton was not the only major performer whose solo career started at The Count House. Michael Chapman, who would later record four albums with EMI Harvest, made his first appearance as an itinerant in 1966. Michael: *I went down to Cornwall with my then-wife in a half-hearted attempt to put my marriage back together. We ran out of money, but then one Saturday night when it was raining I followed a van with a folk club sticker in the back window to the Count House. Ian Todd was on the door and he asked me for half a crown to go in and I did n't have it, so I said I'd play something instead. And I played a Jimmie Rodgers song, a Big Bill Broonzy blues and 'Around Midnight' by Thelonius Monk...*

Andru and Michael Chapman at a photoshoot in Cot Valley, St Just 1969. The dress by Gina Frantini was Michael's 21st birthday present to Andru.

Michael was twenty-five and, after moving on from skiffle, had paid his way through six years at art school in Leeds before becoming a lecturer in photography: *Leeds was a jazz town. So I had started with New Orleans jazz, then worked through mainstream, then hard 'bop'. I used to play with anybody that would have me. Some nights I got £7 a night playing with the Kenneth Baxter Orchestra. We played society balls and hunt balls and on that circuit. The guitar bought my education. We were all beatniks then, with long sloppy sweaters and tight jeans. The great unwashed. But Leeds College of Art had the best staff from Terry Frost downwards. In fact I got an amazing education.*

Des Hannigan recalls Michael's first appearance: *We would get lots of youngsters who were Donovan look-a-likes. Mike was there wearing a Donovan hat and leather jacket and dark glasses and I thought: 'not another one'! Mike in his usual way mumbled a bit behind his glasses. But actually his playing was absolutely stunning. Never heard anything like it.*

Michael: *To my delight Ian said why don't you stay here and play five nights a week? So I borrowed a fiver off him and I stayed for about five weeks altogether. It was very sociable. Everyone got on with each other. It was a hassle-free existence. I'd spend all day on the beach and play in the evenings at the Count House.*

Cot Valley near St Just, its beach strewn with smooth granite boulders, is one of Michael's favourite beauty spots, and somewhere that he later returned for a photoshoot with Andru (see picture): *That summer I lived in an A35 van with my wife. We'd go down and park it up near the beach in Cot Valley and sleep inside it. There wasn't enough space inside for the guitar so I would put it in its case under the van. And one night the heavens opened, and when we woke up the whole place was*

Michael Chapman playing at The Count House during his first summer in Cornwall (1966).

floating in water, including my guitar which had floated away and stuck on a rock! FCHTC

Then at the end of that first summer Brenda Wootton adopted us and gave us a room in her house. It was tiny rabbit warren of little rooms. Typical Cornish house. Sue was there too and was still at school. She was 15 or 16, so about 10 years younger than me. The ultimate piece of jailbait really!!

The success of the Count House had surprised everyone. Then, in 1967, so did its closure. Brenda and John the Fish had started to play in venues far from Cornwall, often calling in on Bedminster Down Boys Club and the Troubadour in Bristol en route. Fish: *Alex Atterson played at the Count House during its second year. He was instrumental in getting me and Brenda to go up to sing in East Anglia. Alex used to run a club in a pub called the Black Horse in Norwich. From there he got us into clubs in Bury St Edmunds, Sudbury and Peterborough. He organised a tour of the whole area and we went there a few times.*

Brenda had this mini-traveller and I used to drive us up there with just the guitar and a change of clothes. I did all the driving. Brenda was a terrible driver. Once we took a wrong turn off a roundabout and she stuck it straight into reverse and backed onto the roundabout again!

Everyone assumed we were married. She used to call her husband Woottie - she would say 'I've left Woottie at home' - and it would dawn on the organisers that we were n't actually married. And of course they'd arranged for us to have a double bed!! But we did often share the same bedroom.

We were at Radio Norfolk one time just about to do some recording when Alex turned up with a letter addressed to us. He said 'I'll give it to you after the show'. It turned out to be a letter from J Ian Todd that he was closing the Count House. We felt he never had the courage to tell us face-to-face. He had to wait until we'd gone away. To me it was a bitter blow that came out of the blue. It had been such a successful venture.

I stayed on an extra week in Norwich. Brenda came home. Poor old Derek Brimstone who is a comedian - it was his night at The Count House when it was formally announced that it was closing down and he

87

had to try and get people to laugh, poor bloke. But Brenda was determined that we would continue so within that very week she secured the church hall at St Buryan, and the club became Piper's Folk at St Buryan. It was at St Buryan for two years and then it moved back to The Count House again.

The impact of the closure was lessened by the fact that, by 1966, several other venues were running folk music events. Martin Val Baker: *The Penmare at Hayle put on the likes of T.V. stars Robin Hall & Jimmy McGregor and Nadia Cattouse, and in Penzance Tel Mann had his Tell-a-Tale Club.*

West Briton, May 1966. The Penmare Hotel folk club ran for a couple of years, having been initiated by Matt Cogan . The Jayfolk were schoolgirls from Truro who included Jill Johnson, later of The Famous Jug Band.

In the autumn of 1966 I arranged a series of folk club gigs at the Winter Gardens dance hall in Penzance. I signed up traditional singer Peter Chatterton from Sheffield, singer/guitarist from Falmouth Vernon Rose, and a friend of Donovan, Iris Gittens, who sang and played very much in the Joan Baez mould, as residents. Each of the resident singers earned £3, Pete acted as M.C. as well and we padded out the night by encouraging visiting musicians to do a floor spot.

The next step was to book guest acts through contacts with a London agency. Our first name act was the top English singer and banjo player Shirley Collins who cost all of £10 - but that included her return train fare from London, and accommodation at £1.

Folk singer and painter Jonathon Coudrille and his Rolls Royce in the mid-sixties.

I went to meet Shirley from the London train to give her a lift to the venue in my old van only to find that Jonathan Coudrille who was due to do the support had turned up in his sparkling white vintage Rolls Royce. Sheepishly I had to ask our star how she would like to travel and got the expected reply!

89

Chapter 6: The Folk Cottage

The Count House in Botallack provided the blueprint for another celebrated folk club some 30 miles further east. John Sleep was working as a chemistry teacher in Newquay at the time: *John Hayday and I would go to the Botallack Count House in 1964 - 65 because it was the only thing around. Roads down there were very slow - right through Redruth and Camborne with no dual-carriageway. We'd sometimes sing two sessions down there. On Friday 7 to 11 then 11.30 to 2, then come home and go and do it again on the Saturday. It was crazy. So John and I thought it would be better to set up a club up here.*

The year was 1965. *John had a friend called Willoughby Gullachson who had a farm. He had a barn which we had to convert ourselves. We put in a staircase and made it sound, and I had to do the electrical wiring and get it registered as habitable. There was a big fireplace downstairs and eventually there were stairs inside and out. People coming to the cottage would pay at the door and I used to collect the money. The Elsan chemical toilet was in a shed on the opposite side of the courtyard. Next door there was a well and the toilet got emptied down the well!*

Jane Sleep is John's wife: *I made the sandwiches - cheese or ham sandwiches - in my comparatively hygienic home, then took them to the club. Making them there doesn't bear thinking about! We had to take containers of water up there as there was no running water.*

Benches were school issue - like the sort you'd have in a school gymnasium. A Newquay artist - who owned the island - did a mural of a naked lady on the wall behind the stage. She was in silhouette. It was his idea to do it - and his paint.

John Sleep and John Hayday at the Folk Cottage. The corrugated asbestos roof and distinctive painted mural of a naked woman turning away from the viewer; are just visible. Photo John Langford.

Fish: *It was a wreck of a cottage. They had to put another layer of floorboards on top of the floorboards that were already there just to be safe. They would light the log fire downstairs and the room upstairs would fill with smoke!*

The club was not easily accessible and John Sleep worked hard to bring it to people's attention: *I recall putting up advertisement boards on the Gannel stretch - the road leading into Newquay - about who was going to be at the Folk Club. The council threatened us with legal action over those boards, it was a real struggle. People would drive out to us, and leave their cars in the lane and they'd be backed up the road all the way to Mitchell. There was also some parking in the field opposite.*

Drugs did n't really become a big feature of the place. It was so wholesome you wouldn't believe it. When the children were small you'd be fine with leaving them downstairs. There were hotel workers who'd come there for the second session after their work, and there were families. It was surprising. You got all the generations.

John and I started as the resident singers and we'd get anybody else we could to sing. I was teaching so quite a few were youngsters from the school. My stuff came from the EFDSS, and local songwriter David Dearlove. And I also sang Cyril Tawney songs because our voices were similar.

John and I also had a group of people we would book from up-country. They would get off the train at St Austell or Truro, and stay with us - on a 60's style push up couch in the front room. If we could afford it we would feed them and give them bread and breakfast and maybe £20.

John Sleep recalls some of the visiting performers: *Gerry Lockran was always good. He had a terrific presence. He really took on the persona of the blues man, with snake hips and belt! Pete Stanley's banjo playing was fantastic. And I'll always remember John the Fish doing 'The Wild Coast'. John had a very plaintive voice and it really fitted.*

Ralph McTell also played at The Folk Cottage, having been introduced to Cornwall by Wizz Jones. He would eventually settle and live here.

Born Ralph May in December 1944, Ralph is slightly younger than fellow Londoners John The Fish, Wizz and Clive Palmer. He had grown up in Croydon, in South London and at 15 left school, which he hated, to join the army, which he hated more.

Ralph McTell outside the Folk Cottage, probably 1967

After leaving the army in 1960 he returned to college in Croydon and started playing the guitar more seriously. He had become friendly with music enthusiast Henry Bartlett, and remembers visits to clubs in Soho, and also trips to Eel Pie Island where he met Eric Clapton.

Early in the 60's Henry started a folk club called 'Under The Olive Tree' in a coffee bar in Croydon. Wizz: *The first time I recall seeing Ralph was when I was resident at The Olive Tree. It was a great meeting place for all musicians. Loads would drop in, like Long John Baldry, Bert Jansch and Alex Campbell. Eric Clapton and the rest of The Yardbirds were often there too. Ralph was just starting out then. I remember he was extremely shy and nervous…*

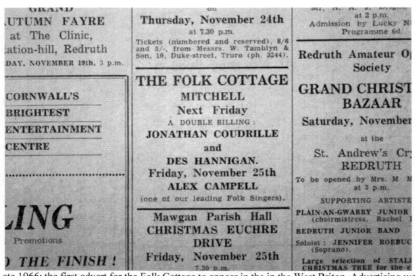

Late 1966: the first advert for the Folk Cottage to appear in the in the West Briton. Advertising was mainly targeted at holiday-makers, and so the local press was only used intermittently.

Henry Bartlett accompanied Ralph on a number of trips abroad, the first one in 1961 a failed attempt to hitch-hike to Greece. Ralph managed to get to Greece via Yugoslavia the following year, however, despite contracting dysentery en route. Like Wizz and Clive Palmer, Ralph travelled extensively in the early 60's and learnt to busk to survive: something he repeated in the winter of 1965 in Paris, when he stayed in the run-down beatnik Hotel du Commerce on the Left Bank. Whilst in Paris he met his future wife Nanna Stein who was from Norway (see photo). He also had a busking partner called Bunny Doyle. Like Wizz Jones and Clive Palmer before them, they would play to the cinema queues. Ralph: *We became on passing terms with some of the old winos up at the Place Contrescarpe. We were all stunned to learn one night that one of them had frozen to death on the street the previous evening...I began to form the idea of a song about the poor people of Paris – I put the song on hold for a while but it never left me.* That song later became his big hit: Streets of London.

94

Nanna Stein originally from Norway.

In 1966 Wizz had acquired a Thames van that he planned to use to return to Cornwall with Sandy and his two little children. Wizz: *When Ralph got back from Paris he was also playing some brilliant ragtime guitar in the style of Blind Blake. He didn't have many gigs on at the time, so I said 'well come down to Cornwall with us'*

Ralph: *I well remember that drive to Cornwall sitting on a basket full of nappies and baby clothes in the back of their Thames van with the kids jumping around and me wondering just what I had let myself in for! On our arrival at Wizz's favourite camp site we had a hasty rehearsal and commenced working.*

In the summer of '66 Ralph, not yet a pro musician, found work where he could. Ralph: *First of all I was on a caravan park called Sun Haven Valley....it's still there. I had an idiot staying with me, who got really drunk and made a fool of himself in the bar and he got us thrown off the site. I used to play there at the caravan park two nights a week in return for having a caravan there (see picture). I was also working there as a general cleaner. In fact I remember I was cleaning the Gents toilets when the World Cup was taking place in 1966!*

As planned Ralph and Wizz also played regular slots in the pub on the beach in Porth: *We played in The Mermaid in Porth until we were banned because too many people came. It was a residency that lasted a few weeks. We didn't have a microphone at first, but it was extra-ordinary. People kept pouring in. We earnt three pounds a night. Wizz insisted on splitting it 50:50 but I said 'no – I'm on my own you've got two kids. You have two pounds, I'll have one'. So here I was playing with one of my guitar heroes, learning all sorts of songs and learning to sing harmonies. It was funny playing in hotels with Wizz where a few years earlier he would have been refused admission. Times really were a-changing.*

Ralph and his caravan in Sun Haven Valley.

Ralph's set at the time was mostly made up of American folk songs: *My preferred style was finger-style guitar-playing which is more intricate than flat-picking. It was songs by Patrick Sky, Tom Paxman, Bob Dylan and some old blues things. But I was also playing a couple of Bert Jansch songs. He was always one of my guitar heroes but at that stage we hadn't become close friends.*

Originally from Finsbury Park Mick Bennett had, that summer, started working as a chef at The Atlantic Hotel in Newquay. He'd hidden in the toilet in order to avoid ticket inspectors on the train from Paddington, and arrived penniless in Newquay. Once there he'd befriended a certain Barney Potter who was able to bring him food from the kitchens of The Edgcumbe Hotel where he was working as a waiter.

As described in his memoirs Mick met Ralph McTell for the first time on one of the beaches in Newquay where they shared a joint. Then one night Mick visited The Mermaid: *We arrived to find Wizz and Ralph playing outside in a large beer garden behind the pub…Wizz was playing his version of Blind Boy Fuller's 'Weeping Willow Blues'. Sometimes they swapped spots, other times they played together as a duo. Ralph's rendition of Bob Dylan's 'One Too Many Mornings' went down well but the small crowd really loved it when they played Guthrie's 'Pastures of Plenty' as a duo with some wonderful country flat picking from Wizz and some great gob iron (mouth organ) work from Ralph. Wizz was sporting a beard and horn-rimmed glasses which never seemed to sit right on his nose. He was forever pushing them back up in mid-flight. He looked like no one else I knew….*BTG

The next time Mick saw Ralph, Henry Bartlett was with him, and they asked him if he'd be interested in forming a jug band. Ralph: *I formed a jug band because I couldn't find anyone good enough to play proper instruments! But my friend Henry Bartlett, who introduced me to tons of music, played the jug and Micky Bennett, who was a really great character, I gave a washboard and tried to teach him to play. Frankly he was the worst washboard player in the world, but the effect was so funny on stage. We've got loads of tapes of people just roaring with laughter at the antics. Then Bob Strawbridge joined us on mandolin. He was about 5 years older than us and a fine mandolin player. Slowly we built up a nice little band. It was fantastic.*

The Folk Cottage Jug Band or 'Mitchell Minstrels' L to R: Lenny, Henry Bartlett, Ralph McTell, Mick Bennett and John Sleep on stage at The Folk Cottage. (photo probably 1967)

That day the newly-formed jug band busked on the beach. But Wizz and Ralph had also been encouraged to get involved with The Folk Cottage. Wizz: *John Hayday came down to The Mermaid and introduced himself and said 'we've opened a folk club…'*

Mick describes approaching The Folk Cottage for the first time together with Wizz, Henry and Ralph in an old post-office van that Ralph had bought in Cornwall. It was mid-August: *Halfway down the lane Ralph stopped the car saying, 'listen to that.' We all stopped and listened to a slice of rural loveliness. The light was just beginning to fade and the air was absolutely full of birdsong mainly coming from the hedgerows above us. John Hayday, all ruddy face and black beard welcomed us at the door and said 'if you intend to play you don't pay'.*BTG

That night Ralph and the jug band, which came to acquire the nickname 'The Mitchell Minstrels' played a lively set and John Sleep, obviously impressed, was keen that they become more involved. Accepting the invitation, Ralph found a way to live on-site: *I found a caravan at the back of the Edgcumbe Hotel which had been standing there for years, and we made an offer to the bloke who owned it. It*

leaked. It was made of hardboard and it had a canvas roof, but he said
I could take it away. So one sunny day John Hayday towed it
to Mitchell. It had no brakes, and it fell off the trailer and went flying
down the road. But there was no traffic in Cornwall in those days
and we were able to pull it out of the ditch and drive it on.

Ralph McTell playing at The Folk Cottage

Jug player Henry Bartlett eventually became involved in running the
club using the contacts he had in London and he lived, sporadically,
with Mick Bennett in Ralph's caravan. In fact, apart from the odd
winter break in London, for the next three years The Folk Cottage at
Landrine would become Mick's home. Whilst there he would act as
caretaker to the club, read avidly, write poems, have love affairs, play in
the jug band, and save the money he earnt in the process in an old
biscuit tin buried underneath an oak tree near the stream.

John Sleep: *The Jug Band started around Ralph, and it was always tremendous fun. It centred itself in the caravan across the road from the folk cottage. And, having very little else to do they used to practice and play there a lot, and used to put on their performances in the evening.*

Starting with Cliff Aungier on 13th January, guest artistes from outside Cornwall were booked every weekend throughout 1967 at the Folk Cottage, as reflected by ads placed in the West Briton paper. Mick Bennett was particularly impressed with Diz Disley: *His guitar playing a la Django was nothing short of far-out phenomenal. His between-songs soliloquies were a joy, with health advice and asides on the general absurdity of life.*BTG

Ralph and Mick visiting Gelbert's farm just up from Willoughby's. Mick, Ralph and the others were allowed to use their phone.

There was snow in the early part of 1967, and in March the oil tanker Torrey Canyon hit rocks near Lands End. Mick worked as a volunteer to help clean seabirds blackened by the oil. He then moved into another nearby caravan owned by the farmer, Willoughby, and Ralph returned with his wife Nanna and newly-born son, Sam.

A young DJ called John Peel was working with a pirate radio station in the North Sea, from where his influential radio show was broadcast between 12-midnight and two in the morning. It was a show that was popular with several of the club's performers.

Ralph: *Mates would come round to the caravan and we'd all listen to John Peel's Perfumed Garden. We enjoyed the music. I was one of the few who thought that John Peel didn't always get it right, but he certainly got it right as far as the Incredible String Band (ISB) were concerned and we found it all very inspirational. ISB had an huge influence on us down here because these instruments were organic, the roots were fascinating, a mix of American, North African and British plus a heavy LSD vision. They were expanding your thoughts and playing instruments that weren't always in tune, and the harmonies were approximate but there was a spirit there which we found totally elevating.*

Summer 1967 was the boom year for the Folk Cottage and the summer that probably changed my life! Wizz persuaded artist Mac McGann to design a poster for the Folk Cottage sessions (see photograph). *By now an all-nighter had been added to the timetable which was to take place every Friday after the normal Folk club session at midnight. My name was included - Wizz insisted on changing it from May to McTell - together with the Folk Club resident John Sleep.*

Wizz agrees: *The really big year in Cornwall was 1967. Pete (Stanley) was back in the UK and it must have been 1967 when we mainly played at The Folk Cottage as a duo. We used to travel around Newquay in the van putting up the posters for the shows: sticking them on fences, trees and lamp-posts. We would also cover the van in posters, and one day in Fore Street somebody knocked on the door and asked if they could buy one from us!*

Pete Stanley: *I remember it was bring your own beer at The Folk Cottage. People would bring those ghastly big tin cans of beer: Grotneys (Watneys). But our gigs were popular. The place was jampacked.*

We'd have played a similar set to the 16 Tons album, and some of our own songs too. I stayed in a caravan at Brighton Cross, with Wizz and his wife and child. We would meet up with Ralph on the beach in Newquay.

Wizz: *When we had the Folk Cottage all-nighters in 1967 the surfing crowd were more or less the same crowd as the Soho hippies and beatniks and musicians there wasn't any real divide. They all used to come to the all-nighters.*

Ralph: *Wizz and Pete were highly accomplished. They were the most professional duo around. Superb. And we got some other fill-in gigs around the place.*

Wizz Jones and Pete Stanley at The Folk Cottage. Photo: John Langford

John Sleep, hailing from Cornwall, had not had first hand experience of the blues being played in Soho: *Our stuff was from the skiffle days and from EFDSS, so the blues and the blue-grass that Wizz and Pete played was a real eye-opener to us. We didn't know that skiffle <u>was</u> blues: we didn't know about the source of skiffle.*

Fish: *Wizz, when he was playing with Pete Stanley, used to flat-pick. Flat-picking is using a plectrum to pick with. Jack Elliott paved the way. It was a country style. Finger-picking was more of a negro style. Pete and Wizz were great buskers. But they were like chalk and cheese as people really. Pete was so cool and laid back and he used to sing and introduce songs in a strong American accent. And when he came off stage he didn't know quite when to drop the accent again! It was quite funny.*

102

Poster designed by Mac McGann

Ralph: *It was the summer of the Sergeant Pepper album: the revolution had taken hold and the music was incredible. There was a sense of change in the air and a true feeling that music was helping to change*

103

the world. I first heard Sergeant Pepper on a portable stereo gramophone up under the cliffs in Newquay. Somebody had bought the album and we were sat there listening to it with our mouths open.

By coincidence, in September, The Beatles came to Newquay to film material for their surreal and largely improvised film 'Magical Mystery Tour'. Many of the outdoor scenes were filmed in Cornwall; particularly in the Newquay area and on Bodmin Moor. Ralph remembers it well: *Brightly coloured signs were hastily painted and placed at strategic points on the roads proclaiming 'Magical Mystery Folk Club - this way!' The Beatles didn't make it to the Folk Cottage - they wound up at Watergate Bay instead - but the Melody Maker reporters did! So their feature on the Beatles became one on the Folk Cottage instead!*

Ralph had begun writing his own songs, and it was through a contact at the Folk Cottage that he was ultimately given a record contract. Ralph: *John Sleep had a friend called David Dearlove who had been working as a music publisher before dropping out of the rat-race and moving to Cornwall.*

David was friendly with the head of Essex Music – a publishing company that at the time had The Rolling Stones, The Who and The Moody Blues on its roster: *Before 1955 I'd been working in a music publishing company called Southern Music, and somebody who worked for the same company was a publisher called David Platz. When I left London in 1962 I remained in contact with him. Eventually he started his own music company (Essex) and was very influential.*

David Dearlove had originally entered the music industry as a songwriter: *I wrote a lot with John Dankworth for Cleo Lane. One was called 'Let's Slip Away' which featured in the film 'Saturday night, Sunday Morning'. Then, coming down to Cornwall, I wrote far more songs afterwards. John Sleep, John the Fish and Brenda all sang my songs.*

David was particularly impressed by the embryonic 'Streets of London'. Ralph: *One day David asked if one of the songs I was playing was my own. He said 'it's rather good you should send it to someone'. So I sent a bunch of songs to Essex music on David's recommendation.*

Wizz Jones and Pete Stanley at The Folk Cottage. John Sleep is playing double bass in the background.

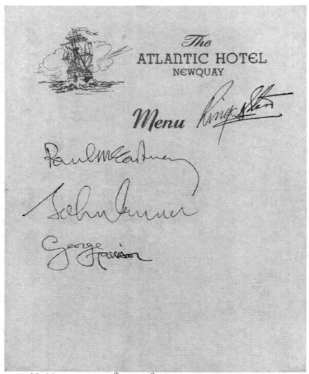

The Beatles stayed in Newquay on 12th and 13th September 1967, filming material for 'Magical Mystery Tour'. Mick Bennett had worked in the kitchens of The Atlantic Hotel during the previous year.

John Sleep: *I remember him singing 'Streets of London' to me and I said 'I don't know about that one Ralph...'. He played it to Jane and I at the cottage in Crantock as an embryonic song. He was a breath of fresh air to us, because we hadn't really heard that type of thing.*

After his 1966 season at The Count House Michael Chapman returned to Yorkshire and, determined to become a full-time musician, gave up his post as a photography lecturer: *Because I'd been playing 6 nights a week in Cornwall to people from all over the world, I thought I'd get lots of gigs. But in fact it was difficult at first...*

His career - which in some ways mirrored Ralph's – also started to take off in the summer of 1967 thanks to their mutual contact at The Folk

Cottage. Michael: *It had happened to Ralph about a month before. David Dearlove was a talent scout for Essex Music who were publishers that also had a 'recording arm'. He just said to them 'you've got to check this guy out'. I'll be forever grateful to him. At the time I hadn't started writing songs, they just wanted me as a guitar player. Essex Music paid for me to make a record then eventually leased it to EMI. It took quite a while to put the deal together. By the time it was time to go into the studio I'd written a whole bunch of songs, the floodgates had opened. I realised I could write!*

David Dearlove: *There were other terrific people, like Wizz Jones, but Wizz seemed rather established, whereas Ralph and Mike were young and just beginning. What impressed everybody was their great expertise on the guitar, and a terrific ability to do melody, particularly Ralph.*

Mike Chapman (left) in bishop's robes during Coverack carnival, here with Andru and Norfolk-based Alex Atterson. Mike and Andru often stayed in a camper van at a country club nearby in Pedn Vounder. Alex founded the Norwich Folk Festival, and organised tours for Brenda and Fish.

107

I remember the Folk Cottage as if always bathed in a warm glow. They used to have a fire there, and in the winter you'd come in out of the cold and into this lovely warm, welcoming place...

The summer season 1967 marked the first of many return visits to Cornwall for Michael Chapman: *I came back every summer for ages. I'd play at the Folk Cottage for a week, then The Count House at Botallack for a week then I'd move out to the Lizard and play in a country club in the restaurant at Pedn Vounder, down past Goonhilly.*

Guitarist Pete Berryman, originally from Newquay, was a new arrival at The Folk Cottage in 1967. Here he would play both as a soloist and a member of the jug band.

Originally from Newquay, he had left Cornwall in 1964 with his pop-band Shaun and the Shondells. Living in London they made a single with EMI and played widely including support slots with bands like The Who. During this time, however, Pete had become more interested in folk: *When I was still living in Newquay there was a telly programme called Hullabaloo hosted by Martin Carthy. It featured one guy playing an acoustic guitar and he was like a whole band in one person. That guy was Davy Graham, and after Elvis he was the next major influence on me.*

Pete played with London-based folk band The Haverim for more than a year, but when they broke up he returned to Cornwall: *I got a job as a porter in the Edgcumbe Hotel. After my first night a funny-looking bloke appeared: 'I'm Barney - you couldn't lend me your shoes could you?' It was Barney Potter who played in Ralph's jug band. He took me out to the Folk Cottage and that's when I met Henry and the others.*

At some point during 1967 a regular visitor by the name of Paul Drake made a film at the club featuring a cardiganed John Sleep together with John the Fish, Gerry Lockran and The Mitchell Minstrels. As well as capturing the live performances, it includes shots of the café space downstairs, complete with open fire, tatty soft furnishings, and non-alcoholic refreshments.

Stills from Paul Drake's film of the Folk Cottage

Pete Berryman's band The Haverim, though based in London, played at least twice at The Count House in 1966, and once at The Folk cottage in 1967

Chapter 7: Donovan returns to St Ives

Early in 1965 Irish singer, Noel Murphy, who became a regular performer and resident in Cornwall, found himself at the helm of a folk club influential in the careers of many of the emerging singer-songwriters: *I was in the Scot's Hoose one evening with Derroll Adams - American banjo player - when we were approached by a nicely spoken young man who said 'Mr Adams I'm opening an all-night folk club in a basement in Greek Street and I was wondering if you'd like to compere the session. Derroll said: 'No. People won't pay to see me falling asleep, what you need is Murphy here'. And so I became the first resident at Les Cousins, and I used to run Friday nights. The guy's name was Phil Phillips, and the club was run on the door by Andy Mathews. His family are referred to in Cat Steven's song 'Mathew and Sons'.*

Les Cousins was part of the expansion of the folk circuit in the mid-sixties and, though small, it attracted some very big names. Noel: *It was tiny, about the size of a single-decker bus. It was a dry club, so people would just drink coffee there. Donovan was one of the St Albans crowd, like Maddy Prior and Mick Softley. He used to get up onto the stage - which was about the size of a pool table - and I'd introduce him. There was a corner of the stage that I'd keep for myself about the size of a telephone directory, and the place was so crowded I'd be there with my chin on my knees, all crunched up just two feet from people like Bert Jansch, John Martyn, Davy Graham, Paul Simon and Jackson C Frank. Jackson was my favourite of the singer-songwriters and he used to come with his then girlfriend Sandy Denny.*

At the time Paul Simon wasn't famous. But Simon and Garfunkel became famous when they were in England. Their record company had taken 'The Sound of Silence' and added strings and an arrangement, and it became a world-wide hit.

Nick Drake used to come down to Les Cousins with John Martyn. John was a very wild man but I could handle him, and he and Nick were good friends. John took me to one side and said 'On no account are you

111

to ask Nick to sing as he is painfully shy and won't have the bottle'. So he would just sit there and take it all in instead. He had a tragic life but is now I think better recognised.

By summer 1965 Donovan had had two top ten singles, and had released his first album: *I got to know Donovan very well, and we used to go to his recording sessions. I became his minder for one or two gigs. He's got one withered leg, and a club-foot. He was doing a tour of big theatres and asked me to accompany him. The tour was headlined by The Byrds, and bottom of the bill was 'Them' from Belfast.*

Around the same time Donovan returned to Cornwall to make the first of two films. He had received extensive press coverage, some of it, however, challenged his authenticity as a folk singer and compared him

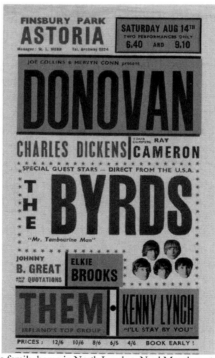

Close to Mick Bennett's family home in North London, Noel Murphy acted as Donovan's minder at this gig.

112

Donovan seated with guitar on Porthminster Beach, St Ives. Jane Val Baker is standing to the left of the photograph. (Photo: Martin Val Baker)

unfavourably with Bob Dylan. Perhaps this was not surprising. He'd not been playing guitar for very long - nor had he had much in the way of life-experience.

Ralph McTell: *In 1965 I was playing on the streets of Paris with this other guy and we started to play Donovan's 'Catch The Wind'.....well I'll be honest - me and my mate used to take the mickey a bit, because Don was foisted on us by the media and many of us would much rather have seen Bert Jansch in that position....Don was a kind of amalgam of The Clancy Brothers and Bob Dylan and Woody Guthrie with his 'This Guitar Kills' instead of 'This Guitar Kills Fascists' - and I have to be honest, there was resentment from those of us who had already been playing that music for some years.* website

In 1965 Jill Johnson first started going out with future Queen drummer, Roger Taylor. Both of them were teenagers living in Truro. Jill would later sing with The Famous Jug Band: *I really liked Donovan. I remember him as one of the first British contemporary folk singers to make that cross over to the 'popular' music side. Prior to that it all seemed to be only the Americans who could bridge that divide with artists like Joan Baez, Peter, Paul & Mary, Judy Collins, Leonard*

113

Donovan singing to Linda who after marrying with Brian Jones of the Rolling Stones eventually became his wife. In the film they and other 'beats' appear to sleep rough in the WW2 bunker above Porthminster Beach (on the St Ives side).

Cohen, Bob Dylan etc. He was the first one to make British folk 'cool'.

In the early 70's Jill's friend and singing partner Sue Johnstone went on to set up the Queen fan club: *Although we never performed it in public, I know that I played and sang 'Catch the Wind' - probably just Sue and I playing around. The folk clubs that we played at in those days - 1965, wouldn't have been tolerant of songs that contemporary – though they did get better pretty quickly after that – especially when Dylan went electric.*

In January 1966 an hour long documentary was broadcast on ITV. The film boosted Donovan's credibility, by giving him a back-story in which Cornwall looms large. Called 'A Boy Called Donovan' it was shot in atmospheric black and white, and has very little dialogue, other than Donovan reciting verses of his own beat-poetry. It depicts him and his ever constant companion, Gypsy Dave, leaving the bustle of London, and living on the beaches of St Ives with a band of 10 or 20 other beatniks. They sleep rough, eat mackerel cooked on an open-fire, play guitars and smoke joints, before returning to London for a party (see photos in chapter 4).

Martin Val Baker, resident in St Ives and son of writer Denys, was drafted in to help stage what proved to be a unique and fascinating re-enactment of the beatnik lifestyle. It was a film which also featured another habitué of Les Cousins: *Donovan, who remembered my sister Jane from earlier days, sent the film crew round to hire us all as extras. Eventually a dozen or so of us gathered on Porth-minster beach with Don, his friend Gypsy Dave and also the American folk legend Derroll Adams who was travelling with the party. For three pounds a day, good money then, we were to play beatniks, sitting around a camp fire cooking mackerel and potatoes whilst Donovan mimed to a tape of his current hit record 'Catch The Wind'. The props department rushed around town buying kettle, mugs, cutlery and rolls of tin foil, all of which was in mint condition and so we had to age it all with the aid of candle smoke. As for the mackerel, well there just weren't any in St Ives on that day so the company had six driven over from Newlyn by taxi.*

Filming continued for a week, on the beach, in an old Second World War bunker above it and in the woods above the town where Don and his friends had camped first time round. The continuity girl would demand 'who was smoking in the last shot?'. All our hands would shoot up and we were tossed Senior Service cigarettes, a posh smoke that no self respecting beat would have been seen with in those days.

Martin Val Baker and Tinks (June Stone) also listen to Donovan singing in the bunker on Porthminster.

115

Still from 'Wear you love like Heaven' (1967)

It was to be one of the last and most memorable depictions of the British beatnik. As 1966 continued, following drug-busts and appearances in the Bob Dylan film, 'Don't Look Back' Donovan's material success made his image as a down-at-heel traveller untenable.

But fashions were changing anyway and, like the Incredible String Band, he was adopting the more colourful foppish clothes of the psychedelic era. The beatniks were becoming hippies, and this more flamboyant Donovan, came to be a strong influence on Marc Bolan of T-Rex, amongst others.

In late 1967 Don travelled to Cornwall again to make another promotional film completely different to the first. The director was Karl Ferris who that same year helped Jimi Hendrix find a more confident brightly-coloured afro-haired look and went on to design posters and album covers for him.

The film is more than 15 minutes long, during which time four of Donovan's songs are heard, including the eponymous 'Wear Your Love Like Heaven'. Filmed in West Penwith in and around the open-air

116

theatre on the cliffs called The Minack, it has no dialogue, but there are some ambient sounds - like waves and seagulls. Mixing fey medieval symbolism with dreamy psychedelic imagery it is reminiscent of films by American underground film-makers like Jack Smith or Kenneth Anger, as well as a number of other more mainstream films.

Still from 'Wear you love like Heaven' (1967) depicting Donovan in The Minack Theatre

We see Donovan in grainy black and white riding on a horse through some woods, then dismounting and arriving at a deserted beach. Wearing beads and long flowing robes he discovers a cave, which he enters. Inside are two children playing pipes. The three of them go outside again and the film fills with intense colour, as they run joyfully across the beach, playing at the water's edge. At one point they hold up four kites pulled from the sea that together spell out the word 'Love'.

Donovan's first visit to Cornwall in 1963 had been a rite of passage for him, marking the point at which he turned from a naïve adolescent into a self-styled troubadour-poet. In 1967, when he also performed at Brenda Wootton's new club, he had returned as a fully-fledged star.

117

Donovan at Pipers, St Buryan. In the background is Noel Murphy. Photo Sue Ellery.

Chapter 8: Piper's

The new club in question was Piper's Folk, and Brenda opened it in May 1967, a few weeks after The Count House closed. Sue Ellery: *I think Brenda had 3 weeks notice. Though she was away at the time she was determined that it wouldn't close; that it would reopen the following week without a hiatus somewhere else.*

Brenda speaking in the 80s: *We were on BBC television in Norfolk one night and when we came out Alex (Atterson) gave us a letter each from Ian Todd and the letter said 'very sorry The Count House is closing'. We had to sing in Great Yarmouth that night and we had become very fond of what we were doing and Fish was hopeless. He said 'I'll 'ave to go back to fishing'. We was having a big rave up at the end and Alex said to me 'you can't let this stop you Mrs Wootton you go home and you find somewhere'*

I met the committees of the church and the chapel and whoever wanted to know. They said 'you aren't going to want alcohol are you?' I said 'there's no need we never have had it'.

Ralph McTell compered the first evening and 280 people turned up. And Mike Chapman sent a message saying he couldn't get down because he was singing in Scotland. But he got in his car after and he drove all the way down and he arrived about 9 o' clock with his eyeballs out on stalks. FCHTC

Sue: *She was a strong character even then. She didn't have the confidence she had in later years but when she decided she wanted to do something she did it. She came back and instantly got on the phone. She phoned everyone she knew, phoned all the village halls and finally found St Buryan. She went out there, set it up, got in touch with all her music friends to arrange singers, refreshments, speakers and lighting and whatever else. So one week the Count House closed and the following week Piper's opened.*

I'm proud to say that I was the one who came up with the name. 'The Pipers' are two standing stones near St Buryan. The stone circle known

119

as 'The Merry Maidens' was supposed to have been girls that were dancing on a Sunday, and hence were turned to stone, and the Pipers were playing for them.

Donovan playing at Pipers in St Buryan. Photo Sue Ellery.

Brenda chose an image of the Greek god Pan, god of nature and music, to symbolize the club. Sue: *Not sure where she got that from. I think it was chosen because he is piping. Later there was also a big piper's figure that used to sit at the back of the stage. She would have drawn it on a big sheet of hardboard and father would have cut it out and she would have painted it.*

Mike Sagar: *Brenda by then had caught the bug, and was reaching the peak of her powers as a performer and organiser. She had the energy of five men, and she could really bring people along with her.*

Sue: *Pipers did end up six nights a week. It was fairly intensive. She would book a guest artist for the week and they would come and play every night. There was some kind of arrangement that they would do Friday at the Folk Cottage. When they came down they generally stayed in our house at Leskinnick. When we started at St Buryan Ralph was one of the regular performers. He got paid £3 a night I believe.*

Donovan's friend, Noel Murphy was another of the guests. Noel: *Brenda was a massive influence on Cornish Folk. She would open Pipers' for six nights a week and she had her favourites and I was one of them. And another was Mike Chapman. Brenda would organise things for you. You didn't dare interfere! You'd be told 'you're doing a week here. You're coming down on the 26th August and you're doing The Folk Cottage the week later, and also the Swan in Wadebridge'.*

Fish: *It was interesting. The people who went to the Count House went to St Buryan but said it's not as good as the Count House, and the people who went to St Buryan went to the Count House and said it's not as good as St Buryan.*

There was a totally different atmosphere in the two places. One was a huge great big church hall. The Count House was small by comparison. In fact there was a two week period when St Buryan was pre-booked in the summer and it had to go to Lamorna. Donovan sang at Piper's because Noel Murphy was booked, and he'd come to look up Noel.

Noel had given up his residency at Les Cousins in 1967 in order to tour more widely across the country. He describes the unique atmosphere of the Cornish clubs at the time: *Piper's and The Folk Cottage had something special going for them. Firstly there were families on holiday which I love. Only 40% were local. So in the summer people would come straight in from the beach, they'd be suntanned, their hair bleached by the sun, and they'd be wearing shorts and sandals. In London the audience was quieter, especially for acts they didn't know, which gave the impression that London audiences were a bit cold.*

Folk Cottage and Pipers 'folk families' meet. Wizz, Ralph and Pete Stanley at Piper's with Brenda and John the Fish behind them. Just visible is a small version of the Piper's emblem on the wall.

Michael Chapman also has fond memories: *The first time I played the song 'Rabbit Hills' was at Piper's in Buryan. I'd just written it and was really pleased with it. It went down really well.*

Mike Sagar: *In the Summer I was resident in the folk clubs and I used to accompany Brenda. I'd go to Leskinnick Street to rehearse with her and go there after the club on most nights. She didn't seem to need sleep and she'd always have a tray of cakes. I don't know how John put up with it. He had a day job!*

Fish was her first accompanist, then Brenda did a lot of material with Mike Chapman when he came down. It was fabulous. She loved jazz, and Mike was so clever.

Michael Chapman: *Brenda and I shared a love of torch songs: long, slow ballads by Julie London and Peggy Lee, and things that came out of jazz. I was used to backing jazz singers and Brenda knew a lot of those songs, so we'd do gigs in restaurants together. We used to gigs at The Quiet Woman in St Ives. But it wasn't a big deal.*

122

Brenda and Fish at Piper's in St Buryan. Probably July 1967. The notice behind them reads 'Next week: Steven Benbow'. Photo: Sue Ellery

Sue Ellery bottle-feeding Ralph and Nana's son Sam in the front garden at Leskinnick Street.

As she had in 1966, Brenda provided accommodation for Michael Chapman and Andru. Mike Sagar: *Mike (Chapman) stayed at Brenda's house for a few weeks at a time. She put everyone up. The house wasn't very big. But it became full of 'folkies'. If a whole lot of people came down some of them would stay with me. Decameron used to stay with me.*

Sue: *Michael Chapman became like a member of the family. The Yetties from Yetminster, Dorset also used to come down every summer. One summer they spent a week stripping plaster off Mother's front-room wall. She had decided she wanted to take it down to the granite, so they were there scrubbing it all out with wire brushes! They also used to go on picnics with us on Hayle Towans (see picture).*

Mike Chapman: *Brenda used to go down to Harvey's in Newlyn and get half a dozen crayfish and half a dozen bottles of wine and that was the picnic!*

Andru remembers another picnic with Brenda: *It was one of the summers when everyone seemed to go down to Cornwall. It was a hot summer and we were all down on the beach one day, with Ralph and Nanna and Sammy their son, Michael and Alex Atterson. Everyone was stripped off and having a great time except Ralph who hates the sun and was sitting there fully clothed in 95 degrees and we finally persuaded him to take his shoes and socks off and he got sunstroke on his feet!*

Folk hearthrob Gerry Lockran also stayed with Brenda in September 1967. He was on a tour of the West Country with a young musician by the name of Mike Silver who had, that summer, just 'gone professional'. Later Mike would accompany Brenda on a tour of Germany. Mike: *I went to Jersey with a bag and a guitar and I slept under a boat for a few days. Gerry had the best gig on the island at a bar called the Caribbean Bar and I got to know him there. He was a really charming man and at the end of the summer he said 'I'm going to Cornwall for 10 days. I'm doing a tour and if you want to you can come with me and I'll make sure you get some gigs'.*

A day-trip to the harbour at Lamorna. L to R: Sue, her then boyfriend Jan Yeates, Brenda, Mick Bennett, John Ellery, Nanna. Below: Ralph with Sam's baby bottle nearby.

He brought me down in his Triumph Herald. And he was an awful driver. Gerry was one of those drivers who would start telling you a story, and slow down whilst he was talking. So we'd be doing 30 mph on the main road, and he would be completely oblivious. But he was one of the biggest pulls on the folk scene at the time.

We played The Folk Cottage, Pipers, Plymouth, Barnstable, Exeter. In those days you'd go and do the gig, then you and a bunch of the audience would go back to the organiser's house and there'd be another session until God knows how late in the night.

Mike Chapman, Andru Chapman and Alex Atterson on Hayle Towans

And Brenda was a great hostess. Top brick off the chimney. You got more to eat than you could shake a stick at. She was very, very generous. She would always have something special on a Saturday night after a gig. She'd get back before anyone else and she'd be in the kitchen with two loaves of sliced bread making fresh crab sandwiches, or cheese and ham, or whatever.

Her husband John was a lovely guy too. He was a sweetheart. He had the patience of Job and you needed it to be with Brenda!

Brenda was an extremely charismatic person. Like anyone that charismatic she was n't the easiest of people to be with, but she carried the Pipers Folk Club. It didn't matter who was booked to play. People came because Brenda was going to be there. Piper's ran 7 nights a week in the summer. It was packed.

Sue Ellery: *When the club was at St Buryan, Westward TV made a short film with Ralph Bates who played Warleggan in Poldark. Part of the film required a choir to be watching from the Minack Theatre above Porthcurnow Beach. Somebody asked Brenda to get a group of people together to sing in the film.*

Shot in almost the same locations as Donovan's, it was called 'Mayday Mayday' and was by director John Bartlett. Charlie Bate, star of 'Oss Oss Wee Oss', and Cyril Tawney can also be heard on the soundtrack. Sue: *We had the folk club on the night before. Brenda said to the audience if you want to be involved bring your sleeping bags, we'll stay in the club overnight and we'll be down there for dawn the next morning. Noel Murphy was the guest that week. Mother made a festival stew, which meant that everybody brought something and threw it in the pot. Everybody had a big plateful of stew and then we bedded down for the night in the hall.*

Noel went to sleep stretched out flat on a trestle table with the top hat perched on his belly. As I recall he also had his flies laced up with a piece of string with a small bell hung at the bottom!

Fish: *I remember it well. We stayed up all night at Pipers, St Buryan, entertained by Noel, trooped off to Porthcurnow in time for the sunrise only to be greeted by thick mist. There we sang 'Lamorna' to death, Noel making up new words.*

Noel: *We were there at the Minack at dawn. I remember peering over the edge of the cliff at first light, and because it was late summer the water was full of sharks.*

R to L Brenda, Andru Chapman, Sue Wootton, Michael Chapman with guitar and two others (unknown) Probably Hayle Towans.

Another picnic on Hayle towans: The Yetties, Mike Chapman, John The Fish and Sue Ellery also pictured.

Jan sticking up v's to the camera. Ralph McTell seated with Sam, Nanna, and two unknowns early morning before filming Mayday Mayday. The man with his hand raised, Fred Wright, took many of the photos in this book.

The LP 'Pipers Folk' was recorded and released in 1968. Featuring a cover design by Brenda's brother, it is a confident, though understated, collection of sixteen songs performed by Brenda and Fish. Around half of them are American folk songs, including the well-known 'Stagalee', and the less well-known but very striking 'Far Side of the Hill', which Brenda had learnt from visiting singer Tod Lloyd. Most of the others are contemporary songs by the likes of Ewan McColl, and locals Mike Sagar and David Dearlove.

Piper's had a reciprocal relationship with The Folk Cottage thirty or more miles away. Mike Sagar: *It was a drag of a journey but we used to go up to the Folk Cottage quite a bit.*

He explains a fundamental difference between Piper's and The Folk Cottage: *Brenda was from a different generation. We (Piper's) were*

129

*more formal. The evening was set up properly and organised with a
level of professionalism. The Folk Cottage was well run, but perhaps a
little looser. There were jam sessions in the Folk Cottage, more than we
did. Jam sessions are more informal, and less planned. Sing-a-longs
were a feature of the Folk Cottage, but the Pipers' was bigger. People
didn't need encouragement to sing. They were bloody good. The
volume of noise was really quite something. Cornish people are good
singers and they're good part singers too. They can find the harmonies
easily. They're like the Welsh only better!*

Pipers Folk (1968). Cover design by Peter Ellery.

In 1968 Noel Murphy formed Draught Porridge with Davey Johnstone
and Ron Chesterman. Ron had recently left The Strawbs. Davey, who
was then still an inexperienced teenager, went on to play guitar with
Elton John, and has done ever since. Noel: *I was told when I was in a
club in Fife that there was this boy-wonder banjo player. It was Davey,
and about 3 months later he turned up at my house, and came along to
a gig with me in Enfield.*

One of the Pipers' audience members was inspired to open her own club on the cliffs east of The Count House. Chrissy Quale: *I was 15 years old when my family moved from the Midlands to Cornwall. My father, Eric Quayle wanted to write and subsequently published 13 books in his lifetime. The house we bought was Carn Cobba out on Zennor Head.*

I was 16 when I opened the Mermaid Folk Club in 1968. The club was housed in a small barn separated from the Gurnard's Head Hotel and was open every Friday night. I used to print up flyers, which I distributed to people on Porthmeor beach on a Friday morning, walking up and down amid the tourists and sunbathers. Also posters, which I put up in St. Ives, Penzance and St. Just.

There was always a great atmosphere in the club. It had fishing nets around the walls, and was candlelit and very Cornish. The car park on a Friday night was often full, as was the club. Des Hannigan, who also played at Piper's Folk club in St Buryan, Mike Chapman, and singer songwriter Roger Brookes (sadly now passed away) all performed regularly.

Chrissy Quale photographed as 'The Mermaid of Zennor' in about 1968.

American folk music and, increasingly, original contemporary songs, were typical of an evening at Piper's and The Folk Cottage. But in 1968 a club with closer ties to the EFDSS, and therefore to the English tradition, opened. The first recorded club night of the Bodmin Traditional Folk Club was on 31st May. Then in 1969 it moved to the Garland Ox, where the first guest was club favourite, and Davy Graham's singing partner, Shirley Collins.

Indifferent to the emergence of the folk-inspired singer-songwriter, traditional singing continued in a range of settings outside the clubs. Cadgwith, on The Lizard, is well known for The Cadgwith Anthem, a song recorded by Peter Kennedy in 1953 and Steeleye Span in 1975. Sue Ellery: *Buller (otherwise known as Richard Redvers Arthur) and Hartley Tripp were the two most well-known and loved of the Cadgwith singers when I used to go to the pub there with Brenda. The local gig club later named their boat 'The Buller'.*

Brenda adored a good pub sing, and Cadgwith was (and still is I believe) one of the best. Hartley and Buller were superb, and the

132

harmonies were fantastic. She would get completely absorbed in the singing and loved to be one of the crowd, just joining in when appropriate. She loved the atmosphere, and the fact that it was done by and for the locals, not the tourists...

Pipers itself moved back to Botallack on March 29th 1969. Sue: *Ian Todd had this idea he was going to run a discothèque and he had The Count House painted orange. It was horrible! And after a couple of years it closed. So then Mother went back there.*

29th March, 1969. The opening night of Piper's at The Count House. John the Fish, Brenda, John Wootton and Mike Sagar return to the venue of the original club.

Ralph back at The Count House. Behind him are the sinister legs, hooves and tail of the giant piper figure.

Noel Murphy performing with Davey Johnstone at Piper's. Davey later became a guitarist playing with Elton John, Meatloaf, Alice Cooper, Leo Sayer and others.

Chapter 9: Clive Returns

In his humble caravan back at The Folk Cottage, in autumn 1967 Ralph McTell had contemplated giving up his career as a musician.
Ralph: *There were no flush toilets at the farm in Mitchell. There was just a milking shed, a portable Elsan and one cold water tap!*

Jane Sleep: *Ralph and Nanna had our son's pram and we did their washing. We were all newly out of college and university, and life seemed simpler then.*

His new-found responsibilities still weighed heavy. Ralph: *Now we had baby Sam it was clear I had to do something. We were placed on an emergency housing list, and moved back to Croydon where we got a council flat and I applied to start teacher training. I had good intentions, though I was slightly depressed about it having had so many years of freedom...*

However, very soon after being accepted onto the course, Ralph was offered a recording contract through Essex Music: *Suddenly I found that I was getting gigs and having to do the two things at once. Travelling round the country then getting back in the early morning and going on to college, I was falling asleep in class. At the end of the first year I said to my wife 'what do you think?' and she said 'well you've got to do music'.*

A recording made in Cornwall helped clinch the deal, and the song in question took its title from local slang for holiday-makers: *I wrote 'March of the Emmetts', which was a comic song. I'd learnt the word here in Cornwall, and Matthew's Cafe in Newquay was mentioned in the lyrics. The audience responded really well and there was a lot of laughter on the recording, and it was laughter I think that helped me get the contract with Transatlantic Records.*

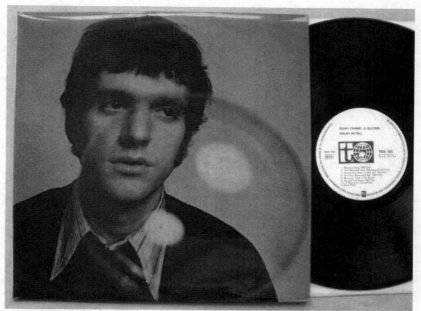
Ralph McTell's first album: 8 Frames a Second

'March of Emmetts' was never put on vinyl, but a number of other songs on the first album, including the instrumental 'Willoughby's Farm' were also about Cornwall: *The Mermaid and Seagull is the most famous one. It was requested all the time. It's a song about people sitting about talking rubbish in a pub, and me going out and wandering off on my own and imagining that I can hear the mermaids and brass bands and all those Cornish-type things as I strolled along the beach. It was popular, so it appeared on the first album together with a bunch of other songs which David Dearlove had heard me play.*

On a couple of the tracks recorded in October '67, Ralph was joined by members of the jug band: Bob Strawbridge, Henry Bartlett and Mick Bennett. Between them they create an earthy, driving skiffle-beat in contrast to Tony Visconti's smooth string arrangements apparent elsewhere on the album.

As Ralph's career started to take off, such that he spent less time in Cornwall, so Pete Berryman became more involved: *Summer 1967 Ralph was resident but by the following winter Ralph had gone and*

137

John the Fish and myself were the resident singers. We kept The Jug
Band going without Ralph, and we got Fish in and it became 'The
Great Western Jug Band (GWJB)'.

I also did solo spots, accompanied a female singer, jammed jazz
standards with Michael Chapman and improvised poetry and music
with Jim Higgins, a young American working in Newquay.

Michael Chapman: *Me and Pete used to sit and play jazz things out of
the top of our heads - just completely improvisational. The folk cottage
was thriving. How people could find it I don't know. It was in the
middle of nowhere and you couldn't get in there it was so packed.*

The GWJB in its various incarnations played in a few venues. Pete: *I
remember a lot of toing and froing between the clubs. Brenda would
come up and sing (at the Folk Cottage). I remember, to us she seemed
ancient! Then Saturday nights me and Mick and John Bidwell and Tim
Wellard - Little John and Big Tim - would go down to Buryan in my
Moggie van and get really pissed in the pub where they filmed Straw
Dogs then go across to Brenda's club.*

Pete Berryman, Mick Bennett and Henry Bartlett: The Great Western Jug Band. Mick's
customized washboard is sitting on his lap.

138

*She loved us really, but we'd wind her up and play something com-
pletely inappropriate like Rock 'n' Roll. It was very informal and we
didn't get paid...Then we'd have more to drink and drive back right up
through Cornwall - me driving really pissed to St Austell then Newquay.*

John Bidwell and Tim Wellard were local lads who'd attended
Newquay Grammar School, and as guitar players they had been regular
patrons of the Folk Cottage.

John had gone to Bradford University to study Industrial Chemistry, but
his academic career didn't endure. Mick Bennett: *The pull of the guitar
and performing with his old school friend Tim Wellard was to prove a
stronger influence. John wrote the song 'He Never Came Back' one
desolate dawn on a deserted platform at Truro railway station on his
way back home from dropping out of University. Not long after this he
took a job for English China Clay as a chemist.*

Fish: *Henry Bartlett used to help run The Folk Cottage. He would book
people and do the advertising. It was a very loose arrangement. A
committee used to run the folk club on a Friday night. Henry the Jug
would put on Jazz events. It was a venue that people could use - by
having a word with Willoughby.*

Pete: *Henry started booking people like Ron Geesin who was a
performance artist doing absurdist comedy, and all kinds of people like
Mike Chapman and Johnny Silvo.*

Mick Bennett assisted by providing a caretaker role whilst living in the
caravan on site: *I improvised a shower from a length of hosepipe given
to me by Willoughby's Dad Mr Gullachson. It was connected to the
outside tap and curled up on top of the barn roof where the sun hit it
first thing in the morning...It worked remarkably well, the warm water
lasting about five minutes, gradually turning to cold then to freezing so
in fact by then you got used to it.*

Returning to Cornwall during summer 1968, Ralph spent time sketching
out ideas for a second album, and for a while living near to Wizz's old
busking partner, Clive Palmer. Ralph: *By that time Clive, founding
member of the String Band, had moved to the same field in Mitchell,
virtually. He took over Willoughby's caravan. Willoughby had had two
years of brucellosis and was as ill as can be, but he managed to keep*

his 6 cows together but finally he got beaten and he rented the caravan to Clive, Mick Bennett and John Bidwell.

Ralph's second album was recorded early in August 1968. It was titled 'Spiral Staircase'and it included contributions by Pete Berryman, Henry Bartlett and Mick Bennett. Ralph: *My residency at the Folk Cottage had sent my writing in its usually two directions, on the one hand ragtime, or good-time jug-band music and on the other a reflective nostalgia for the positive aspects of my childhood.*

John Bidwell and Tim Wellard. Both local boys, they had a long involvement with The Folk Cottage.

Streets of London, the first song on the album, falls into neither of the above categories, however.

Have you seen the old man
In the closed-down market
Kicking up the paper,
with his worn out shoes?
In his eyes you see no pride
Hand held loosely at his side
Yesterday's paper telling yesterday's news

So how can you tell me you're lonely,
And say for you that the sun don't shine?
Let me take you by the hand and lead you through the streets of London
I'll show you something to make you change your mind

140

Ralph McTell had started writing the song whilst busking in Paris, not London, and had offered it to John The Fish to sing the previous year: '*I was a little hurt when he declined the number on the grounds that it was a bit sad!*'. Derek Brimstone, another visiting musician to Cornwall, adopted it instead, and encouraged Ralph to play and record it himself.
sleevenotes

The album was well-received and it led to radio play, particularly on the Saturday day-time show 'Country Meets Folk', and also on evening shows like 'Night-ride' and 'Top Gear'.

Before ending up at the Folk Cottage in 1968 and shortly after making The Incredible String Band debut album in 1966, Clive Palmer had gone hitch-hiking across the world: *I went off to India within a few months of making the recording. That lasted about a year or so. The route I took was through Holland, Germany, Greece, Yugoslavia, Syria, across the desert to Baghdad then to Basra then by arab dow to Abu Dahn in Persia, then diagonally across Persia to Mershad, then from there to Afghanistan, Pakistan, and India. When you're travelling long distances in places like Iran you just sleep on the side of the road. You might have some food with you and you light a little fire. And the next day you carry on. It's a simple existence.*

Whilst in India Clive performed, with his banjo, on Indian television, and on returning to London briefly formed a duo with Wizz Jones. Wizz: *Around this time I was gigging with Clive at places such as Les Cousins in Greek Street, Soho. It was there that I met Roy Harper who had recently recorded his first album 'Sophisticated Beggar' for producer Pierre Tubbs. Pierre had told Roy that he was looking for artists with original material to record for Liberty and United Artists records. Roy's retort had been 'Pierre why don't you record some original people like Wizz Jones and Clive Palmer?' So that was how I got to make my first solo LP.*

The collaboration actually resulted in two LP's: 'Banjoland' a Clive Palmer album on which Wizz played, and 'Wizz Jones' the Wizz Jones album on which Clive played.

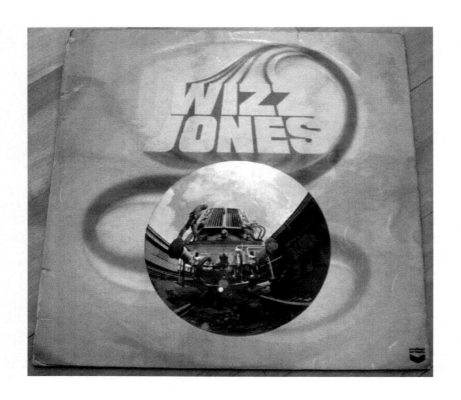

Wizz: *I persuaded one of my old busking friends Long John Baldry to write the sleeve notes (see Chapter Two). It was also the first time I recorded the fine Alan Tunbridge song 'A Common or Garden Mystery' with Beverley Martyn and it was my plan to make that the title of the album. However I was over-ruled and also persuaded to climb on to a diesel engine at Clapham Junction for the photo shoot...*

Ralph: *I think I first met Clive before Cornwall. After Wizz and Pete split up, Clive and Wizz formed a duo and played on 'Country meets Folk', and there are a couple of tracks from the BBC. So I met him in London. That year Wizz and Clive did gigs as a duo at the Folk Cottage and they were fantastic - they really were. I got to know him better during '68 when living in the field.*

Having already visited Cornwall on a number of other occasions, Clive Palmer had returned again, and this time he stayed. *I'd come down to see a friend of mine in Helston, and I stayed there for a couple of weeks. Then the caravan at Mitchell became vacant because Henry Bartlett moved to a flat in Penzance, so I got the caravan and I lived there. That was opposite the Folk Cottage. And John Bidwell came and shared it with me.*

Clive enjoyed the rural environment of the Folk Cottage: *It was quiet and idyllic all week, then at the weekend it went crazy. The guy at the local pub, if you took a large bottle, would fill it up with beer for you, and you could take it with you. Beer was 10p a pint then. The main road went through Mitchell, and you went down this lane to a place called Landrine and you were there. You wouldn't recognise it now. In those days it was a beautiful place. A wonderful place.*

Brenda Wootton wasn't at The Folk Cottage that much. And they were more 'straight' than we were, if you understand what I mean. We were more bohemian, and they always kept a bit of a distance. In the old days things were different. You had people who liked to smoke dope and those that used to drink. And there was a barrier between the two. Most of my friends were not drinkers. We were more into 'raising our consciousness', not getting legless. There was a definite split. And long hair was still an issue here in Cornwall. You wouldn't get served in Newquay in some restaurants and bars if you had long hair...

Jane Sleep remembers Clive moving to The Folk Cottage at Landrine: *That was when my husband John started worrying about whether drugs were going to come into it. It was dodgy because John was teaching, and he was introducing pupils from the school to the club. But John was protected by his innocence. We all knew that Mick was high as a kite when he was playing in the jug band. You don't have to be fully in charge to play the washboard!*

Ralph recalls the origins of one of the bands Clive formed in Cornwall: *Tim Wellard and John Bidwell played on stage at the Folk Cottage before I left. So I knew John as a really hard-working guitar player, who was determined to get on. He became quite accomplished and fell under the spell of Clive and moved into the caravan with Mick. Let's be frank about this, there's no denying, there were drugs taken! And Clive found a soul brother in Mick and with John who was a very clever boy. They experimented with time signatures, and they bounced off each other very effectively.*

143

Poster used to advertise gigs at The Folk Cottage during the 1969 'season'. Other than a mention of Ron Geeson, no ads were placed in The West Briton during the same period.

Clive has this beautifully simple, almost shaman-like approach to music and art, and he's drifted along carried by music all his life. And there they were trapped together living on potatoes and not much else - dope and hope - and they wrote these songs. And they were strange and rather beautiful.

Mick was a bit of a Jack-the-Lad character but blessed with this extraordinarily powerful voice for the skinny little whippet that he

144

was! He had this massive voice and he was influenced by all the music around him. He started writing poems and reading avidly.

When not reading or writing, during the day Mick would advertise the club to holiday makers in Newquay, as entries in his journal explain: *After the initial embarrassment of knowing you look a total idiot, sandwich-boarding becomes quite enjoyable. I try to make it a bit of a show and it's great for chatting up the chicks. Also Barney P has been fly posting for the late night sessions and putting the word about on the hotel grapevine... The result of all this is that the late night sessions have gone crazy. Last night we turned away at least two dozen people.*

The journal also records Mick's first impressions of Clive Palmer: *Childhood polio has left Clive with a lurching gait; as he walked through the audience and up to the stage, he put me in mind of an old sea dog finally making Terra Firma, walking amongst the land-lubbers after a long voyage. Clive, I thought, could be a character straight out of a Jack London story.*

Michael Chapman, having had three spells staying and playing in Cornwall during 1968, had been signed to EMI 'Harvest', along with Deep Purple, Pink Floyd and Roy Harper. Michael: *We recorded the first album at the back end of 1968, but it took forever to come out because EMI Harvest wanted Pink Floyd's album to be released at the same time. But the Floyd got too stoned and couldn't finish it. And EMI got tired of waiting so they released Shirley and Dolly Collins in their place.*

Michael's first album, called Rainmaker, opens with the driving rock song: 'It didn't work out'. Gus Dudgeon, the producer, later became known as the man who recorded all of Elton John's most famous records: *Gus wanted me to work with London session musicians, and that's what happened on 'It didn't work out'. Gus put that band together. I'd met Clem Clempson in the office. His band Bakerloo was signed to Harvest. They were big name rock and roll stars playing on a song of mine so I was pretty impressed, and we were in the world's most expensive studio. The rest of the album cost £145, that single track cost £1750!*

Michael ended up inviting two friends from Hull to play on subsequent recording sessions. The following year one of them joined David Bowie in 'The Spiders from Mars': *I'd been living in Hull and I used to go down to this guitar shop and Rick Kemp was behind the counter. I'd pick up a guitar and he'd pick up a bass and we used to play together there, and I realised what a great bass player he was. The other guy that used to come in there was Mick Ronson. Mick lived round the corner. He was a gardener working for the City Council in Hull. I introduced him to Gus Dudgeon and Gus introduced him to David (Bowie), and the rest is history.*

Chapter 10: The Famous Jug Band

Since living and working at The Folk Cottage, Mick Bennett had been saving his earnings in a carefully buried biscuit tin in the woods. Then, during winter 68/69, he finally blew it on a trip to Morocco. Whilst he was away Clive joined the jug band, and Mick's place as vocalist was taken instead by a talented female singer.

The Jays in 1966 (probably). Jill Johnson is on the left, sitting next to her twin sisters. Sue Johnson, who later founded and ran the International Queen fan club, is on the right.

John the Fish: *Jill Johnson was younger, and tiny in fact, but had a wonderful voice and she made two albums with The Famous Jug Band which are fabulous - I really treasure those two albums.*

Jill had been at the Girl's Grammar School in Truro. Since 1965 Roger Taylor, the drummer, had been her boyfriend. In fact his new band,

Queen, went on to play their first ever concert in 1970 in Truro City Hall only a few miles from the Folk Cottage. Queen performed in the county regularly during 1969, 70 and 71, and it is likely that all the members of the band visited the folk club as audience members. Their first bassist, Mike Grose from St Austell certainly did, and Roger Taylor is known to have accompanied Jill Johnson. Ralph McTell: *I believe Brian May also came to The Folk Cottage.*

Jill: *The Jayfolk started as The Jays in 1964. I was 14. The first line-up was myself, my sisters and my best friend Sue Johnstone (later ran the Queen fan club for years with her sister Pat). We sang mostly at special events, hotels, concerts, etc. The folk club scene wasn't really established at that time. In 1966 we were on Westward TV Folk Wave series, with Martin Carthy and Dave Swarbrick.*

I met Roger Taylor at a folk concert in a barn, he was with the band 'Johnny Quayle and The Reaction' at that time. In April 1967 both of our bands won auditions for 'Opportunity Knocks'. Also in 1967 my two sisters emigrated to Canada and I brought in Penny North and Josie James, and called the band The Jayfolk.

In 1967 and 1968 The Jayfolk played regularly at The Navy Arms in Truro and the Roseland Inn in Philleigh, as well as a variety of concerts, holiday camps and clubs. In the summer Roger Taylor, with The Reaction, ran a series of beach dances in marquees, and the Jayfolk would provide an acoustic intermission.

I was planning on joining Roger in London (he was at University), so I got hired by the BBC and was supposed to start working for them later that year. Then the Jayfolk played a gig in Wadebridge...

The gig was advertised as the final performance of The Jayfolk. Pete: *There was a concert that we played with Ralph in Wadebridge and we were there having a pint and Ralph said 'she's really good you've got to get her in your band'...*

Clive: *Jill Johnson had a clear voice that was uninfluenced. She just had this very, very, clear voice and I thought 'wow that'd be good'. And it was - as you can hear on the record.*

ETER LING
.... ROGER TONGE
.... IAN PATERSON
PAMELA GREENALL
... SCOTT ROBERTS
BERYL JOHNSTONE
.... ALICE FRASER
.. NOELE GORDON
... VINCENT BALL
... SUE NICHOLLS
... JAMES CHASE
.. DIANE GRAYSON
.. SYDNEY VIVIAN
.. PAULINE BARKER
top playing games
u didn't invite me
o out with you. So
say, say it!

SON
luction

Tonight's Big Film
OUT OF THE CLOUDS
at 7.30

ANTHONY STEEL as Gus Randall
ROBERT BEATTY as Nick Millbourne
DAVID KNIGHT as Bill
MARGO LORENZ as Leah
JAMES ROBERTSON JUSTICE
as Captain Brent
EUNICE GAYSON as Penny Henson
GORDON HARKER as The Taxi Driver
Love or money? This is the question
which faces Leah . . .
A Michael Balcon Production
Presented by Westward Television

10.45 FOLKWAVE
The Sea
with
MARTIN CARTHY
DAVE SWARBRICK
THE JOURNEYMEN
THE JOHNSON GIRLS
and
CHARLIE BATE
Film cameramen: GERRY EWENS,
DAVID HOWARTH
Film editor: ROGER CHARLESWORTH
Designer: GUY BASKIN
Producer: JOHN BARTLETT
A Westward Television Production

11.18 NEWS HEADLINES

11.20 DATELINE
A closer look at one of today's top news
stories

The same quartet appeared on Westward TV as the Johnson Girls. They played alongside Charlie Bate from Padstow.

Jill: *So in Wadebridge I see this group of disreputable looking 'older' guys playing this stomping jug band music. Pete was 23, Henry 26 and Clive around 30 I think. It was Henry that came up and talked to me - he was always the front man. Clive just stood there with that sphinx-like substance-assisted grin on his face, and Pete was shy and didn't say much. Henry said that he liked my voice, and asked if I would be interested in joining their band.*

I was very flattered, and excited. He said they had some gigs at the Folk Cottage coming up (Henry was running the club at that time), and that I should practice with them. I liked Henry instantly, but Clive was scary, and Pete was just intensely silent!

Pete: *When the FJB first got together I remember Clive living in the caravan. It was total squalor...You'd have to drink a cup of tea trying to ensure that your lips didn't actually come into contact with the mug!*

Jill: *The practice I did was with Pete at a cottage that he was sharing at Summercourt. I'd go there in the afternoons and Pete would take me through the songs: 'Black is the Color', 'Saro Jane', 'Last Train' and 'Gone'. Clive was not keen on having a female in the band, and Henry*

149

and Pete were both told that they were not to get involved with me personally!

Jill was still a teenager, and her father held a respectable public office: *The band decided that I should join them on tour in January, so I had to break the news to my parents, and we had all three of them join us for afternoon tea in Truro! Ha! My parents were very gracious to these three men who were going to take their 18 year old daughter away with them! Mind you having spent a few years with Roger - who could frequently turn up in a full length fur coat, ladies and sun hat, and drum kit, asking my dad for a lift to the station - they were used to my less-than-conventional friends!*

Clive was definitely the dominant force. He would argue frequently with Henry and Pete about music, and sometimes about the gigs. Pete was really the only one who communicated with me ... an important fact as I climbed into the back of the little red Post Office van, and took off to London in January of 1969! Very Scary!

The Famous Jug Band in The Highcliff Hotel, Sheffield. Photo Pete Berryman

Pete: *Henry was a promoter and people who had been down like Alex Atterson were able to repay the favour so we had a tour that took us up to London, East Anglia and Yorkshire, mostly sleeping in my Morris minor van. Four of us in there. It was tiny.*

Clive had played with Robin Williamson in Northern England so already knew the area. Pete: *We were looking for somewhere to get some food. Clive said 'I know a great place' and took us to a Salvation Army hostel! It was huge shock to Jill!*

Suddenly out of the blue, The FJB were offered the opportunity to make a record. Pete: *We got the recording deal through Wizz who'd made the record for United Artists. He had met Pierre Tubbs - the in-house producer at Liberty Records - and he had recorded Mick Softley, which is how he met Wizz who told him about us. We went into his office on the way up north.*

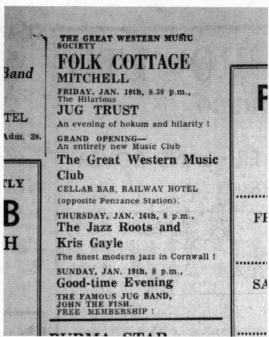

West Briton: January 1969. The Famous Jug Band are booked, by Henry Bartlett, to play at The Great Western Music Club.

The first album 'Sunshine Possibilities' was recorded in the spring of 1969, and released shortly after. Jill: *We recorded most of the songs in one take at the UA studios - all playing at the same time, just as if we were performing. There might have been a couple of extra guitar tracks added separately, but mostly it was as it came. Henry's jug posed the most challenges – getting it not to sound like spitting!!*

Clive: *We got a contract to make that first FJB record, but in those days the financial deals were dreadful. We get a third of 5% each for that String Band record. That shows you what a load of crooks they are! Unbelievable when you think how many copies that first album sold.*

Sunshine Possibilities; the first album by The Famous Jug Band.

Jill: *I think the biggest disappointment for me was the track they chose as the A-side of the single: 'Only friend I Own' rather than 'A Leaf Must Fall'. Not because I was singing it, but because it was such a great song - one of Clive's. I think that might have done really well. Actually, you'd be amazed at how many covers have been made of that song over the years - most notably by Mary Hopkin, who also married Toni Visconti the producer of Ralph's and David Bowie's records.*

'A Leaf must fall' is a song Clive wrote in the caravan at The Folk Cottage: *I wrote it in about 10 minutes. What I do is just muck about and when I find something that works, I then add words to it. It was written on the guitar. The words are based on a Chinese poem, plus just being in that place as well. Cornwall in those days was very different. Most the people you met were Cornish, and the countryside was very peaceful and quiet. Everyone went to bed at 9 o'clock! And when you were away from it you really were away from it. Which is what I've always liked about it.*

Before the album was released in July 1969 - to rave reviews in Melody Maker and The Guardian - Clive left. The other members had decided they wanted to carry on without him. Pete: *I had got together with Jill and that really pissed him off: He said: 'I told you I don't believe in people having relationships in the band'...It got pretty ugly one time and he even threatened me physically - scared the life out of me - though we're still good mates now - but he wanted to move on....*

Clive: *Henry was booking us gigs and making a mess of it, so there was some friction there. He would exaggerate the fee to get us to do the gig. Also Pete and Jill were making decisions together instead of individually...*

At the beginning of August a contingent with links to the Cornish clubs, including FJB, played at the 5th Cambridge Folk Festival. Brenda and John The Fish performed, and the picture taken that day was used for the poster the following year (1970).

FJB without Clive Palmer: L to R: Pete Berryman, Henry Bartlett, Wizz Jones and Jill Johnson

Hippies keep it cool as A scene from the folk festival at Cherry Hinton Hall, Cambridge, yesterday.

John The Fish and Brenda at the 5th Cambridge Folk Festival.
The image was subsequently used for the 1970 poster.

During Ralph McTell's appearance at the festival the audience sang along to one of his own compositions – 'Streets of London', which he'd written in Paris and only performed at folk club gigs. It seems the song was beginning to take on a life of its own.

After leaving the FJB in May 1969, Clive returned to playing again with John Bidwell, Tim Wellard and Mick Bennett. The four of them, based again in the caravan near the Folk Cottage, came to call themselves Stockroom Five.

Mick: *It seemed that Clive and John were constantly playing together, woodshedding as I used to call it, borrowing a jazz term, sometimes playing through the night. Tim and I began joining in with them on these sessions, Tim on guitar and me on bongos, African drum and vocals. Clive would occasionally play the fiddle, resting it upright on his knee and bowing across it Afghani fashion...*

At the time we were playing mainly old timey stuff on stage, but off stage the style of the music was entirely different. It had a distinct Middle Eastern flavour and obviously Clive still had some of the sounds of his Afghani and Indian travels ringing around his head. The overall

155

feel was one of timelessness. Some of it sounds just like field recordings from another age and culture which in a way is exactly what it is COB log

Clive, as the oldest and most experienced of the musicians was the Stockroom Five's natural leader. John: *I didn't feel like Clive's junior at that time, but I wouldn't say the band was particularly democratic: 'mildly autocratic' is perhaps a better description!*

October 9th 1969 West Briton Folk adverts. This advert appeared separately to the main Folk Cottage ad. The previous week another ad had promised Stockroom 5 gigs at The Folk Cottage on Saturdays throughout the winter, however in November the club moved from Mitchell to Rose.

That summer they drove around in his (Clive's) van with a megaphone, and, once again, Mick took to wearing sandwich-boards around New-quay.

The group played regularly at The Wadebridge Folk club, and over the winter took over Saturday evenings at The Folk Cottage. In July 1969 they also put in a one-off appearance at the Interceltic Wrestling Championships in North Cornwall. John: *It was traditional Cornish (Celtic) wrestling somewhere north of Wadebridge. The gig was outside, sitting on hay-bales...*

Stockroom Five and some of the other Folk Cottage regulars also played in Newquay during the holiday season. Mick: *We had a*

156

Wednesday night residency at the Lobster Pot, a club run in a hall in Newquay by a bullish, ebullient Irishman called Larry McLaughlin. We were soon running our own club nights on a Friday evening at the same venue and packing them in. It was the first time I noticed we were attracting a definite hippy-type crowd. Apart from the way they looked, flares and long hair and so forth, the sweet stench of marihuana in the interval was a bit of a giveaway.

West Briton, November 13th, 1969

Clive: *We used to pack it to the gills with tourists on a Friday night. Newquay was nothing like it is now. There was nothing else on and folk was the cool thing. We were playing American old time music: Charlie Pool, Lost City Ramblers etc: old American folk.*

Pete Berryman: *The folk club was in the Roman Catholic Church Hall. One night Larry was introducing them and he made an insulting remark about Clive, and Clive attacked him with his banjo and, effing and blinding, chased him out of the hall and onto the street!!*

The creative squalor of the caravan at Mitchell at the end of 1969 is beautifully recalled in Mick's journal: *It became unseasonably cold. One Sunday morning…I opened the curtains, my hot breath misting up the window…I looked over at Clive and John who were both gently snoring and then at the plate which displayed the remains of last night's chips, stubbed out roaches and fag ends…The gas had run out so I went*

157

*outside to find kindling for a fire, the frosted grass crisp under my feet.
I soon have a pot of water boiling over a crackling fire. I can hear Clive
tuning up then playing his banjo inside the caravan and then the throb
of John's accompaniment. I make the tea and get out the biscuits.* BGT

In fact Mick, John and Clive decided that they couldn't spend an icey
Christmas in the caravan, and so stayed in a squat in Ladbroke Grove
for a few weeks instead. The trip to London marked the end of
Stockroom 5, but also hinted at new musical directions. Mick's journal
continues: *Clive had somehow arranged to meet a friend who was
travelling back from India. He was dressed in full Afghani regalia
including a very extravagant turban-affair on his head. 'I've brought
you a wee bairn' he said to Clive reaching into the sack and pulling out
something wrapped in a piece of cloth. It was revealed....a small, about
2 feet long, Indian hand harmonium. We didn't know it then but in the
near future it would become the keystone of our new sound.* BGT

Recorded with musician –producer Ian Anderson, Wizz Jones' second solo album. The guitar in
the cover photo, owned by Alan Tunbridge, is decorated with fauns and fairies. Other musicians
involved in the sessions included Ralph McTell, Pete Berryman and Ron Geesin.

Although Wizz played some gigs with FJB, he decided he needed to concentrate on his own solo career, and drew on the song-writing skills of old beatnik friend, Alan Tunbridge: *Wizz signed up with The Village Thing label in 1969. He recorded 'The Legendary Me' album, which included eight of my songs - magnificently enhanced by Ralph McTell on harmonium, Pete Berryman on second guitar and John Turner on bass.*

Alan didn't just contribute songs: *I designed the record sleeve using a photograph of my own guitar, which I thought looked suitably mythological. I carried on writing songs as a hobby, and Wizz and a few other performers continued to play them. Wizz's next album 'Magical Flight', with the Plant Life label, featured three of my numbers, and, again, I did the sleeve illustration. A few more songs appeared on subsequent albums 'Right Now', and 'The Grapes of Life'.*

1969 saw new clubs open in Cornwall and old ones move premises. Fish: *The Bodmin Folk Club - still running now - is one of the longest running folk clubs in the country. There was also a club in Wadebridge, and one in Padstow.*

Noel Murphy remembers performing in Padstow: *I played frequently at the folk club in Padstow which was held at The Golden Lion. There was a separate room and people paid 3 or 4 shillings to go in there. They used to keep the 'Obby 'Oss downstairs. Mervyn Vincent was a great friend of composer Malcolm Arnold's and after a gig at the club we went to Malcolm's house. Malcolm was bit of a loose cannon. He wrote a great tune for the Padstow Lifeboat which starts with two very dissonant notes which are supposed to represent the fog horn. There was a great occasion when the brass band played it on the quayside, then afterwards it was all back to Malcolm's garden, for what was a jolly night.*

Fish: *'Room at the Top' in Redruth was run by Dave Penprase (ex-Staggerlees). The club was upstairs and it was bigger than The Folk Cottage. About the same size as St Buryan. Dave invited Long John Baldry and Davy Graham down. I don't know if Dave knew but Davy Graham was on heavy drugs by that time.*

His playing was incredible but he would suddenly stop and there'd be an uncomfortable silence, then he'd start playing something else. Or he

159

would try to play really impossible things, and get it wrong, then try again, and again and eventually get it right and you'd see his face light up.

Then in the interval he went around talking to the posters, and everyone was like 'keep away from him'!

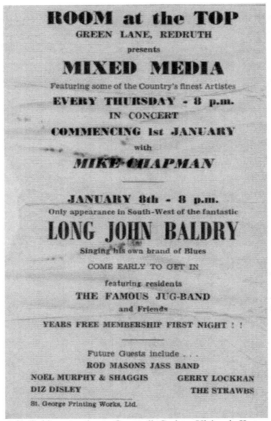

Long John Baldry returning to Cornwall. Graham Hicks via Kernowbeat

I also saw him in Truro. It was his birthday and he was down with some friends and he called in at The Folk Cottage and played a few things.

In the middle of the autumn The Folk Cottage moved from Mitchell. The first concert in the new venue was on November 14th. Fish: *The Folk Cottage moved when Willoughby put his place up for sale and moved to Canada.*

John Sleep: *We moved the club to an old chapel. It was quite good up there. But it was beginning to get away from me because I was teaching and I couldn't keep it going. Ella Knight and John Battensby took it on, and eventually took it to The Swan in Truro.*

Ella Knight (centre) & Carrie Langford (R) at The New Folk Cottage, Rose. Many of the photos pinned to the wall are now in John Langford's collection and have been reproduced in this book.

Tankards in Falmouth was another less-known club active in the 60's. Fish: *Tankards was run by Jim Bassett. Jim was one of the main people behind it. He had such a strong voice for such a small man. Mike Kessell was also involved...*

Chapter 11: Cannabis Creek

1970 marked a watershed year in the careers of many associated with the Cornish folk scene, as a number of them started to make waves outside the confines of the club circuit.

The Stockroom Five's last gigs were at The Folk Cottage before it moved location in autumn 1969. The band had become friendly with two members of the audience: brother and sister Stephen and Demelza Val Baker who lived on the banks of the River Fowey.

Still known as The Sawmills, the house would later become a recording studio where artists like Oasis and Muse recorded some of their most celebrated albums. In the late sixties it was charmingly dilapidated and home to writer Denys Val Baker and his wife Jess, who had left St Ives in the middle of the previous decade. Accessed only by water and nestling in trees, it became a crucible of hippy-style experimental living and music-making.

John Bidwell, the first to return to Cornwall from Ladbroke Grove, stayed with Tim Wellard. Tim was renting a chalet in the grounds. John: *Sawmills was romantic and amazing - most of the time. It was on a beautiful creek backed by magical woods, like a separate little world really. We didn't have much contact with most people of the local village - Golant. The villagers there called it 'Cannabis Creek' and were a bit scared of us I think, except for some old childhood pals of Steven and Demelza. From time to time arty/musicy people from around the county, London and beyond would visit and some would stay for a while.*

I spent many happy hours canoeing up the creek under the over-arching canopy of leaves in the spring. It was very beautiful. Because I was pretty good on the water I usually got the job of rowing us to (and more riskily back from) the 'King of Prussia' pub in Fowey.

Demelza and Denys Val Baker with Sawmills behind them. Photo Martin Val Baker.

Denys was not completely happy to have his home overrun by 'the beautiful people' however, as he describes in his book 'Life up the Creek': *Huge hordes were usually swallowed up into the tiny confines of either Stephen's chalet or the one Demelza now used down on the quay, and all we ever heard - and it was pretty melodious - was the playing of guitars and zithers, or maybe the latest Beatles or Rolling Stones record on the hi-fi...there were times when drawn by the surrounding beauty and a sunny day, various individuals would wander around the grounds and often I would find this rather annoying. Especially when Jess and I slunk to the quay to sit on a big swinging couch we had set up - only to find it completely occupied by a variety of pleasantly relaxed hippies. When I complained to Demelza she examined me reproachfully. 'You're just so possessive Dad. You should give more. Let love enter your soul...you'd better get used to it really because soon I'm going to build a big commune in the woods'*

Tim and John ended up working with Demelza to form The Novelty Band. Amongst the most memorable venues the three-piece played was an open-air medieval theatre called The Piran Round near Perranporth. John: *I played there for several weeks on the trot with the 'Novelty Band'.*

The trio also tried to open a folk club in Fowey, above Jess's pottery, but were refused a music license after a residents' petition blocked their attempts.

Mick, after contributing to a track on Ralph's third album, joined the others at Sawmills along with Clive Palmer. Mick: *I met up with Clive in London and we travelled back down in his trusty old van to good old Kernow. In the right weather The Old Sawmills could be the most beautiful place on earth. After a short punt up the river from the town of Fowey you see on your port side a little creek nestling in a wooded valley. A China Clay railway line runs by the river and as you float under the little bridge you're met with a placid, more thoughtful world.*

Mick, an aspiring writer himself much admired Denys Val Baker: *I remember him fondly as a gentle gentleman who always treated me with the greatest respect which I paid back in kind. I was also aware he had this extra dimension about him.....he had a publisher. He taught me by example that if you want to write you must go about your business quietly, EVERY day.*

March 1970, and a gig early in the year for The Novelty Band playing alongside John the Fish in Stithians near Redruth

The four members of Stockroom Five were reunited, and a new band now involving Demelza, started to evolve. Mick: *If I remember correctly I started to write the lyrics to 'Music of the Ages' in Denys Val Baker's study there. He'd kindly said I could use the room whilst he*

164

was away sailing in Sanu (his boat) and one evening I was whiling away a few hours reading a book from his library, The Illustrated Book of Zen Buddhism, when pictures of sculpted stylised lions in front of a temple caught my eye. What a great name for a band I thought: The Temple Creatures.

Chrissy Quayle was still living near Zennor. She was introduced to his family in Fowey by Martin Val Baker, who had returned to St Ives after a spell in London. Chrissy: *I was invited to visit and I took a small rowing boat down the creek to the house. Denys and Jess Val Baker were away and the house had become a commune, with lots of people and musicians. Clive Palmer and Little John (Bidwell) shared a chalet where most of the jam sessions took place.*

Clive was the most forceful personality in the band. He wrote wonderful lyrics and melodies and was a hard taskmaster, and the band rehearsed for hours on end. Clive did not suffer fools gladly. Nobody had any money and at times survived on tea and potatoes. I remember an incident when Clive returned from somewhere to discover someone had taken his last tea bag. He was furious and berated the culprit for hours, and threw him out of the chalet!

The Temple Creatures, a new group, which was the main attraction at a Guildhall concert last Friday, left to right, John Bidwell (balalaika), Clive Palmer (hand organ) and Demelza Val Baker (bongos).

Possibly taken in Fowey looking across the estuary towards Bodinnick and published in The St Ives Times and Echo; the only known photograph of The Temple Creatures, August 1970. Described as 'a new group' they appear as a three piece with the hand-organ (or harmonium) from India in John Bidwell's lap. They returned to play at The Guildhall in September.

165

I was singing backing vocals with the Temple Creatures and did some gigs, including The Railway Hotel, Penzance a few times, and The Perran Round.

Whilst at Sawmills, The Temple Creatures began to incorporate eastern influences into their music. They also experimented with new sounds. After losing a dulcimer, Clive and John set to work trying to make another. Mick: *The machine heads came from an old guitar, the wire for the frets from the garden shed...Out of an old bone found in the garden Clive had fashioned a one-piece bridge. John then experimented with the angle that the string hit the surface of the bridge at. Eventually he had it buzzing and bright and discovered that bending the string at the right time made it slur and sing. So there it was, the Dulcitar.* BTG

The instrument was completely unique, but it was one of several they constructed in a similar way. John: *It was all pretty rustic, experimenting with instrument-making: bamboo whistles, Clive's rebec, and the dulcitar of course. Probably the main inspiration for the instrument-making was the lack of money to buy instruments! Clive was really the prime mover in that area. He's still very active in instrument-making of course. We weren't aware of other musicians doing this. The dulcitar was an attempt at a new sound, whilst the rebec, which is a type of violin, was an attempt to resurrect the mediaeval sound. (We never used the rebec on stage or record by the way).*

By necessity all the instruments were rather crude. John: *We didn't have a workshop as such, and only a limited range of tools. I still have the dulcitar and the Levin Goliath guitar which we used. The hand organ fell apart. I sold the Salvation Army organ (which we used on Moyshe McStiff) soon after COB finished. I don't know what happened to the other instruments.*

The new band played in venues local to Sawmills, often having to reach them by boat. Mick: *I recall one memorable gig I did with them in Fowey Town Hall. We decided to make more of a show of it. Clive had run up costumes for everyone on Jessie Val Baker's old Singer sewing machine. I remember mine was made from an old white and gold brocade curtain, full-length with a hood. Clive had made himself a rather wonderfully layered flowing arrangement out of dark red linen topped off with a rather splendid turban. Apart from my poetry spot(!) it's remembered as a great night.*

The dulcitar as it is now: original hand-made instrument as used by The Temple Creatures and COB. Photo John Bidwell.

Afterwards we packed all the gear into the Val Baker's inflatable dinghy and just managed to all squeeze in beside it...Halfway back the boat started to deflate and we began to ship water...Clive improvised a bucket from his turban and had to start frantically bailing out water!
BTG

The tranquil environment of The Sawmills inspired Mick to write more poems himself, three or four of which would become songs recorded by C.O.B.: *In spring of 1970 I'd started writing a poem about an old* girlfriend called Mary whilst staying in one of the cabins at The Old Sawmills. I only had a few lines and was walking close by the woods when a magnificently ancient magnolia tree just bursting into blossom came into view. It struck me the blossoms looked like hands clasped in supplication. I found a story in Denys's library about 'Martha and Mary', the daughters of Lazarus and after a week or so's honing, the poem 'Hands of Mary' was born (later Martha and Mary).

Another song derived from a liaison with a dancer. John: We were mainly staying in nearby chalets, but at one point we built two tepee-type structures from tree branches and dried bracken at the edge of the wood further up the creek. I think this gave a few people quite a buzz when they came to visit...

The visitors in question included a visiting American dance troupe known to Demelza. Mick recalls one female member of the troupe visiting him in his tepee: I was laying in the bender listening to Clive and John blowing in the tepee next door whilst I read Rimbaud, as you did. She crawled in through the low entrance tunnel naked except for a blanket. She was holding a small pipe which she passed to me along with a small ball of dark brown gooey stuff. It was opium, my first and as it turned out, last hit of the stuff. The experience inspired more arresting lyrics: 'Rest peaceful, be assured of this, the breath of life is but a kiss'. BTG

Martin Val Baker had been living in London, but when he returned to Cornwall he resumed his work as a music promoter: In 1970 I returned to find the Temple Creatures going already. I put together the Temple Creatures gig at the Guildhall. We closed The Mask Club St Ives, The Railway Club Penzance and Chrissy Quayle's Mermaid Club in Zennor for that night and got 450 in! There was a photo in the St Ives Times & Echo of the Temple Creatures to tie up with the first (of two) gigs. It was taken by their staff photographer at the time.

John Bidwell: I remember at least one Guildhall gig ending on a real high with us and Bob Devereux performing together.

Bob Devereux is an artist-poet who moved to Cornwall in the late sixties: I compered the gigs at the Guildhall. Martin Val Baker organized them. BOCuvM was me and Jim Hughes. Jim had seen the name in a dream and insisted that we used it! We were offered so many *gigs that Jim and I took to the road in the winter thumbing from one venue to the next. High Speed Gas was Don Fowler and Alan Greenall.*

The Guildhall concerts generally finished with a piece of mine called 'Yes, We've Had Some Fun Today'. All the musicians were on stage for 'Fun Today' and the audience sang the chorus. It was a totally improvised piece, with improvised music.

Mike Silver, having visited Cornwall with Gerry Lockran in 1967, had been invited down by Henry Bartlett for a summer residency at The Great Western Folk club in Penzance. He played at The Guildhall in September billed as a 'Fontana Recording Artist'. The recording in question had been made with Mike Beason, and was an unusual LP entitled The Applicant: *The Applicant was like a folk opera and when we did an excerpt from it at a folk club in Croydon Jackson C Frank came up to us afterwards. He knew Alan Paramour and offered to talk to him to see if he could get a deal. So Alan gave us a publishing deal, and his son David produced the record.*

Shortly after the Guildhall gig Mike formed 'Daylight' with Chrissy Quayle and Steve Hayton. They all moved to Earl's Court and secured a deal with RCA for their eponymous album. Chrissy: *When I was 17, I went to see Daddy Longlegs, an American band playing at the Winter Gardens in Penzance, where I met guitarist Steve Hayton. I also first met Mike Silver and subsequently all three of us got together. From the first moment we played together it had a certain magic about it, and that was it....Daylight was formed. We played at Cecil Sharp House and The Roundhouse, amongst other venues.*

Meanwhile, now three albums to the good, Ralph McTell's reputation was growing largely by virtue of the hard work he was putting into touring across the country, though he had also made some appearances on the daytime radio programme, 'Country Meets Folk'. Ralph: *I didn't get that much radio play. But there'd been this groundswell and I was there at the right time. It was largely word of mouth, but don't forget there was this huge network of clubs at the time. John Renbourne introduced me to a northern promoter called Wim White and after the first appearance at his club I got six more gigs. I looked at an old diary the other day. I was working 7 nights a week, and travelling in my little GPO van with a ladder-rack on the roof. I was driving all over the country for six quid a night.*

Poster designed by music promoter, Martin Val Baker for the second of two Temple Creatures gigs at The Guildhall, 1970. Mike Silver and Chrissie Quayle were residents at The Mermaid Folk Club near Zennor, who would go on to form 'Daylight' Mask was a folk club set up in the old café at St Christopher's St Ives by Julie Hewitt.

In June 1970, a few miles from the Folk Cottage, Jill Johnson's ex-boyfriend, Roger Taylor performed in public for the first time with a certain Freddie Bulsara (later Freddie Mercury). His new band 'Queen' had just formed.

But that summer Ralph took part in an equally historic gig. In June at a low-key concert in Ewell Technical College, his support act was the painfully shy Nick Drake. Sadly it would prove to be Nick's last public performance before his untimely death. Then in August Ralph performed at The Isle of Wight Festival. It featured a star-studded line-up including The Who, Miles Davis and Joan Baez, and also marked one of the very last appearances of both Jimi Hendrix and Jim Morrison. Attended by over half a million people, ultimately the crowd was so huge it proved unmanageable.

Ralph: *I was ever so glad I did it, but my only regret was that I didn't get to see Jimi Hendrix at the end of the evening because my manager had sensed that panic was setting in, and the crowd was getting more and more restless. I had to wait a very long time to see how intense people felt about the music. It was the end of something. I saw everyone who played the same day as me. I saw Pentangle, Donovan, Moody Blues just watching from the side of the stage.*

My manager insisted on catching the last ferry back. Bert Jansch was asleep under the stage. I knew Jackie McShee (Pentangle), because she was a Croydon girl and I used to sing with her sister, she watched the show. I knew Danny and John Renbourne by that time. John helped me in the early days. He told people about me.

The speakers and PA were not that loud - nothing like they have now. I didn't even have a pick-up on my guitar, and I had my lucky shirt on which was a red tennis shirt which I had swapped for a set of strings in Milan. The DJ, Jeff Bexter, was sitting on the top of the stage playing records between the acts and I got an encore, and I was waiting to be sent back on. My manager was out the front and I thought 'do I go back what do I do?' I was waiting for someone to tell me. Then Jeff put on a record and my manager, Jo Lustig, rushed out onto the stage in front of 500,000 people and the DJ leant down to listen to him and Jo grabbed him by the beard, and nearly pulled him out of his chair! It was extraordinary.

Ralph McTell entertains an enormous audience at The Isle of Wight Festival.

Somewhere in the crowd that day were Sue Ellery and her parents: *Brenda went to the Isle of Wight with a small camper van which had a tent that fitted on the side, and Father was there too for sure...*

Now 26, Ralph subsequently embarked on his first tour of the US, playing several gigs in New York, and also singing at the famous Troubadour club in LA.

In 1970 the Woottons' friend Michael Chapman brought out his second EMI Harvest LP: 'Fully Qualified Survivor'. It generated a lot of publicity and John Peel named it his favourite album of the year: *When 'Survivor' came out John Peel championed it partly because his wife is from Scarborough and she loved the track 'Postcards from Scarborough'. So I got a lot of airplay not just from John but from everybody.*

The track immediately following 'Postcards from Scarborough' is a short, light-hearted guitar instrumental called 'Fishbeard Sunset': *When John the Fish was playing at The Count House he always had one eye out of the window as we had this tradition that the gig would stop and the entire audience would walk out onto the cliff to watch the sunset, then come back in again and we'd restart. So one night I was sitting to one side of the stage watching the sunset through Fish's beard. And that's where the title comes from...*

The record featured Mick Ronson on electric guitar. Mick had been playing with Woody Woodmansey and Trevor Bolder in Hull band The Rats, and the following year the three of them would become The Spiders of Mars on Bowie's seminal Ziggy Stardust album.

Michael Chapman on the Peter Cook and Dudley Moore show BBC1 1970. Rick Kemp (bass) later played with Steeleye Span, and Richie Dharma (drums) with Lou Reed on 'Transformer'

Michael Chapman: *I tried to put a band together with Mick, but he wouldn't leave The Rats - he only went with David (Bowie) because David took them all, lock, stock, and barrel. I didn't want the others. I thought they were hopeless! They were pretty dire, except for Mick who just had 'star' written all over him. Of course Mick was a bit embarrassed about wearing make-up with David. They all were. They were just beer-swilling blokes from Hull!*

Instead, with TV appearances in the offing, Mike found Rick Kemp and Richie Dharma: *The first gig I did with the band was 'The Peter Cook and Dudley Moore TV Show', which was the biggest show in town, and it just took off.*

We went over to Holland to play a televised concert with Traffic, Frank Zappa and Sly and Family Stone. Traffic only did one song and

174

wouldn't play any more, so we got an hour live on TV that went out to Belgium, Germany, France and Scandinavia and it made us. We just worked there for years on end. I've also got footage of another TV show at Olympia in Paris where our support act was Black Sabbath.

Then Micky Abrahams (ex-Jethro Tull) poached my drummer Richie Dharma. So Rick and I went out as a duo, culminating in my first disastrous American tour in 1971. I did five weeks out of eight. By the time I returned to New York, I hadn't got paid, I'd been robbed at gunpoint, the manager had bailed out, and Rick had bailed out too.

So I was there on my own. From New York I was supposed to go to Chicago, to Denver and to California, but I rang the record company and said 'I haven't been paid. I want £2000 dollars delivered to my room at the Chelsea Hotel by lunchtime tomorrow otherwise I'm going home'. And it wasn't forthcoming so I just said 'bye now'.

I've often wondered what would have happened if I'd made it to California because the singer-songwriter thing was just about to take off over there. Maybe I should have braved it out, but I was in bad condition. I was doing too much of everything and I was broke and leaving a trail of unpaid hotel bills behind me.

In 1972 Richie Dharma went on to join up with David Bowie and Mick Ronson to play on Lou Reed's Transformer album.

During 1970 Ralph McTell and Michael Chapman were not the only Folk Cottage regulars to be touring widely. The FJB were yo-yoing between Cornwall and London, and struggling with some of the same stresses that come with travelling. Pete: *We were in Cornwall when Clive left - and I remember writing the songs for the second album in Cornwall, then in London we had a flat above Bruce May who was manager to Ralph and Wizz and Christy Moore...*

Jill: *In Cornwall, we had our own places, Pete and I in Summer-court, Henry in Penzance ... In London, initially we'd sleep on the floor of Henry's parents' house in Streatham...till they got tired of us.*

The FJB's second album 'Chameleon' was released in 1970. Most of the songs were Pete's compositions, though a cover of Michael Chapman's song 'Rabbit Hills' was also included.

Mike Chapman and band on The Peter Cook and Dudley Moore Show.

The touring continued and the band acquired a new manager, but it wasn't enough and they finally split-up when Jill left in April 1971. Jill: *I got sick – and there was no-one to help. Seriously - it was the only thing that I ever wanted to do. It was great at the beginning. However, it was difficult going from mostly taking the lead in the Jayfolk to being the non-voting, token 'chick' member of FJB. I have a strong personality, and was not used to being in the background. Being the only female member of a band on the road, and mostly 'living rough' was stressful. Also getting involved with another band member was not a good idea, and an added complication. Returning to Cornwall, I completely lost touch with everyone, and they didn't contact me ... so it turned out to be more of an 'end' than a 'rest'!*

Soon after FJB broke up Pete Berryman made an album on Trans-atlantic Records with John James. Pete: *'Sky in my Pie' was released in 1971. I think when we were still in Cornwall we had a different fourth member of the FJB. For a while it was Wizz, then John James was in it. That's when me and John started working together - and we knocked some tunes together for that album. I remember rehearsing with him in Cornwall. For a while he lived in Luckett which is near Bodmin Moor and his mother-in-law had a house there.*

176

Wizz: *FJB had some radio programmes, and they called me in on it but it didn't really work - I wasn't able to add much. When Pete and I made The Village Thing album (The Legendary Me) in 1969 that's when we really got around to playing with each other. He was living in London then and I wish I could work with him all the time because he's such a sensitive musician to play with.*

Chapter 11: C.O.B.

Towards the end of 1970 Demelza Val Baker and John Bidwell left
Sawmills and went up to London - as The Temple Creatures - where
they played at Les Cousins and the prestigious Marquee in Wardour
Street. They stayed in Shadwell with Judith Piepe who was known to
Noel Murphy, and had previously provided accommodation to Paul
Simon when he was living in London.

Mick: *The Temple Creatures were always a loose affiliation of different
people. Both the Val Baker girls and Chrissy Quayle from Zennor were
members at one time or another. Clive left sometime towards the end of
1970, I think. The band carried on for a while but I don't think it was
ever the same without Clive, his input was crucial to their sound and
material.*

Clive went to Edinburgh for a couple of months. When he returned to
Cornwall at the beginning of 1971 he found a caravan in Mylor, a few
miles down the coast from Fowey, near a large country house. Clive: *It
was a Russian émigré from the war who owned the land with the
caravan. It wasn't far from Greatwood - about a five minute drive.
Nelson is supposed to have stayed there. Wonderful spot right on the
estuary, to get there was complicated though: it was in the middle of the
woods!*

At around the same time CBS approached Ralph McTell's manager, Jo
Lustig, interested in signing up some new talent. Clive: *The record
company would say 'we need some folk acts' and Jo would say 'I'll get
them for you'. So Jo would find the acts, record them, and then sell it to
the record company. So it was suggested that we got together because
we'd already played in Stockroom Five in Newquay, then we'd started
writing our own material. So Mick and John from that came in with me
on the C.O.B. thing.*

Ralph had always admired Clive Palmer's music. Ralph: *Jo asked me if
I knew any good acts. I mentioned Clive and Mick Bennett. He knew
that Clive was important because of the Incredible String Band, and he
also negotiated a deal with CBS for three other acts.*

Mick: *In Jo Lustig's apartment in South Kensington, it was all pugs and period furniture. With as little ceremony as possible - I for one only glanced at the contract - we all signed the record deal with Jo and therefore C.B.S. We also signed a management deal, plus I think rather stupidly signed over our publishing to Jo's company. The carrot I think was an advance royalty payment for the princely sum of £500, between us. This may also explain why also we passively accepted Clive's Original Band as the name.*

A contemporary photo of John Bidwell playing the dulcitar

John Bidwell: *Many of the songs on the first album were written over a few years leading up to C.O.B. 'Music of the Ages' may have been played with Temple Creatures, but I'm not entirely sure.*

Clive: *We wrote some of the C.O.B. songs in the caravan in Mylor. Mick would come up with poetry and stuff and so would I. And we would try and put tunes to it and slowly build it up.*

Mick Bennett: *I used to go for long walks and dream up songs as I went. The walks would have been around the coves and footpaths near Falmouth and along the Fal Estuary. It was easier then. There were fewer fences up. I'd sing the tunes to the others and they would work them out. Clive was always extremely good at finding that special chord. John was a multi-instrumentalist, which was a help as my contribution wasn't so musical.*

179

Clive: *So then we went to London. John and I stayed with my father and Mick stayed with some friends in London whilst we were trying to build it up.*

'Spirit of Love' was recorded in May 1971. Mick: *The Marquee Studios in Richmond Mews in London's Soho just round the back of the famous Marquee club in Wardour Street were brilliant. The Temple Creatures had recently gigged in Les Cousins which was just up the road.*

Though they felt at home in Soho, Mick and John were not familiar with recording studios, and the band as a whole were casual in their approach. Ralph: *I must be honest they were so undisciplined - it was a nightmare. I remember having to ask Clive not to sniff when he played the violin because the mic was right by his nose and he'd say 'it doesn't matter, who cares?' Several people told me I was completely mad to do it, but I did have faith in the boys and I'm very proud of what we achieved. The records sold in their thousands all over the world - for which none of us received a penny.*

John: *Ralph has said they were difficult recording sessions. I think he was really referring to the band's lack of exposure to modern technology. Also, we never worked with a rhythm section as such, so tracks could be a bit of a voyage of discovery tempo-wise!*

A small choir which included Chrissy Quayle joined them on one of the tracks. Mick: *Recording 'Wade in the Water' a cappella proved easy, the rehearsals had paid off, but we kept straying off the beat. Enter Beat Meister May (Ralph) who was soon in the booth with us clapping and stamping on a bass pedal. It reminded me of all those years ago at the Folk Cottage when he would take on the choirmaster role for The Mitchell Minstrels!*

We had all the tracks sewn up in four days which left one for mixing. Spirit of Love, as it was a vaguely anthemic track, seemed like a good title so that was decided.

The front cover of 'Spirit of Love' features a watercolour portrait of the three band members: John with the dulcitar on his lap and Mick surrounded by books *(see photo)*. John: *Mick was (and still is) usually in the company of books.*

Mick: *Almost overnight our world changed. Jo-the bread head-Lustig was doing his job. Black Roger became our roady and in his red Volkswagen split-screen camper-van we embarked on a countrywide tour of the clubs. With three or four gigs a week at last we were truly on the road. I loved it, it made us work hard and forget ourselves.* BTG

One of the first concerts was back at the St Ives Guildhall. Martin Val Baker: *It possibly the only time ever that a complete band and their instruments arrived at a gig on two mopeds! It was during that season (1971) and the following one that I teamed up with Julie Hewitt to run the Mask Folk Club at Mr Peggotty's Disco.*

The poster is one of several by Martin that sported distinctive hand-drawn psychedelic designs: *Terry Pascoe, did the Scarlet Runner poster for me around the same time. Despite appearances neither of us ever touched LSD! We would sit in the Sloop drinking beer instead...*

C.O.B. appear at the Royal Festival Hall as support to Clive's old flat mate Bert Jansch. Bert also played on a couple of Wizz Jones albums. Photo Mick Bennett.

A fortnight after their performance in St Ives C.O.B. made the first of two appearances at The Royal Festival Hall. Mick remembers it well: *We went through the whole of our 'Spirit of Love' repertoire, then friends joined us on stage for the encore for which we sang 'Spirit of Love'.*

Clive was undoubtedly the most at home on the concert stage. He had a depth and seriousness about him that I knew I could never muster. John was workmanlike about his task having taken on his usual scientist-working-in-a-laboratory persona!

One of the best gigs we did that summer was undoubtedly Cambridge Folk Festival. I remember feeling that at this time there was a great accord between the three of us, for a while the chemistry in C.O.B. was just right.

In 1972 Jo Lustig secured a second production deal, this time with Polydor. Back at 'Sawmills', where they made preparations, it was decided that Genevieve Val Baker would join the band as a percussionist and Mick would take a more central singing role.

182

Mick: *It was a very confident and happy quintet of C.O.B.s that left for London that sunny Sunday summer·morning in '72. Demelza's drumming had improved a hundred percent in the last year and Genny was forever singing. All things considered we were better prepared for the recording of Moyshe than we were for Spirit.*

June 1971. C.O.B. appear at St Ives Guildhall a few weeks after recording the album 'Spirit of Love'. Poster art and design by Martin Val Baker. Iris is local singer Iris Gittens.

CLIVE PALMER (right) with JOHN BIDWELL AND MICK BENNETT

COB in Melody Maker 4th September 1971. The photo was taken in the garden of a pub in Enfield, near Clive's father's house.

Clive had a great idea and tune for a song, sung as if by a minstrel in the court of King Solomon. We borrowed heavily from the bible for the lyrics. It was decided that for the recording I would sing 'Song of Solomon' which I was very pleased about as I loved the song and the way we were doing it.

I'd wanted to write a song in the style of a traditional ballad for a while. I had extensive notes from an evening spent in Biddy Mulligan's pub in Kilburn a few months before so I used these to help me write 'Pretty Kerry'. A year or so later the I.R.A. were to bomb the place when the guv'nor refused to pay his dues to the boys.

For some time John had been playing around with a riff on the dulcitar. It had what sounded like a circular rhythm, a convolution out of and into itself. Eventually he transcribed it onto the guitar and transformed it into the song Eleven Willows played in 11/8 time. COB log

The album was recorded in the celebrated Sound Techniques studio – which was already familiar to Clive from the ISB sessions: Ralph: *It was recorded very intensely over a few days. I had to wing it and trust my intuition. On Eleven Willows which is an instrumental I got Genevieve, who was playing percussion rather badly, to sing quietly*

184

but she was not at all confident so we had to tweak the vocals. Bert
Jansch recorded it years later. We managed to rescue the 'Song of
Solomon' by getting Danny to play on it. He had brought his young boy
around to see the recording studio, and I said 'You haven't got
your double bass in the car have you? Yes why? This song is a
nightmare it's got two movements in it and we can't get them to stick
together'. Danny roared all over it and helped knit it together, that's
how that track came together.

Mick: *There was a blip or two on the sessions. One in particular was
entirely due to the over use of some rather strong Nepalese Temple
Balls (hash) which certainly didn't make Ralph's job any easier. I
looked over at Clive and became convinced that his head was about to
explode. Meanwhile he seemed to have fallen in love with a rather
gorgeous potted palm. My own head felt like the inside of the bass drum
which Ralph on occasion, I'm sure out of deep frustration, would
peddle the living daylights out of in a pointless effort to make us keep
time!*

Ralph: *Both albums are very otherworldly, but then they were as
people: all three of them were very otherworldly.*

*The dulcitar is a cross between a dulcimer and a sitar so you had a
sitar effect without having to spend 20 years learning to play it!
So you've got this mystical eastern sound to it: strange harmonies lots
of minor keys - and a biblical influence. Mick is Jewish and he decided
he wanted to understand more of the bible and he wrote these lovely
warbling psalm-like songs and Clive put tunes to them and I helped
with a couple as well. This mixture of styles I found terribly attractive.*

Mick: *As far as the album's title is concerned I wanted something that
smacked of a heroic quest; that also reflected our different
personalities. I like a quote from Clive that I've read somewhere that
Moyshe, the album, was 'an attempt to reflect life's spiritual journey'. I
think that's exactly what it was.* COBLOG

Moysche McStiff's gatefold sleeve. The designer Paul Whitehead also designed record covers for Genesis and Van Der Graaf Generator

Ralph: *'The Tartan Lancer' was the name of the off-license at the bottom of my road in Putney. And Mick's jokey jewish title Moyshe McStiff was a combination of Scots tradition which Clive had immersed himself in and a Jewish name. I threw in the sacred heart to confuse it even further. Some American critics have written pages on the title alone! Mick and I still laugh about this now - and one reviewer even read the whole bible before he wrote his first review!*

Mick: *We played Cambridge Folk Festival to great acclaim again but generally we were still struggling money-wise even though we were now headlining most of the gigs.*

Clive: *Then we got a Pentangle tour and that was amazing, that was 1972 and we were making £500 a night.*

Mick *The gigs with Pentangle were a step up again for us and a tour of the nation's top concert halls was timely as to be honest the thought of a career that involved an endless round of folk club gigs just wasn't worth it.*

186

Poster for the 1972 Pentangle tour

It was a real pleasure to stay in decent hotels for a change but of course it came at a price. Jo paid us every ten days or so, and our gig fees that at first looked like a king's ransom soon shrunk to such an extent that we may as well have been back playing the clubs again. Once more disillusionment began to set in.

During the tour the band were reunited with Wizz Jones. Mick: *I'd always felt that Wizz was a slight enigma, remarkable in his attitude towards performance and indeed everything. I thought to his advantage he was never one of the boys. From the outside his life-style always looked exemplary. No drugs or booze, and certainly no womanizing.*

In the New Year (1973) to keep the ball rolling we decided to do a Friday night residency at The Half Moon pub in Putney. Clive: *It built up from nothing: started with ten people then ended up packed.*

Mick: *After just a few weeks it became quite a success but we all knew it wasn't enough. It was on one of these Friday night sessions that the*

187

sails finally fell windless on the plucky little ship that was C.O.B. The next morning, without seeing Clive, I left for Cornwall. In a way I think we knew our time had come and gone.

C.O.B was a mutation, the strange psychic offspring of two bands, the Stockroom Five and the Temple Creatures. Stylistically poles apart, the former was Clive's kindly old timey alter ego, the latter, a kind of group-grope towards some acid-fuelled utopian idyll. Neither stood the test of time, they didn't need to, they spawned C.O.B.

With the help of Ralph McTell we produced two albums with some good songs on them and then it was time for us as individuals to move on. Not so long after this I heard that the Val Baker's were putting up The Old Sawmill's for sale. It really did feel like the end of an era. COBlog.

COB. broke up early in 1973. Clive Palmer now has ambivalent feelings towards the group: *The company were hoping they could exploit my connection with the String Band. Some of the String band stuff was off the map: I couldn't get into it. Even now I can't. I'm not even a big fan of C.O.B. I hardly ever play the records. I like it, but it sounds a bit 70's and a bit naive. We do look a bit silly with those bell-bottom trousers!*

Clive reflects on his short-lived involvement with the three bands (ISB, FJB and COB). *It's enjoyable as long as you're not arguing too much. It's hard to keep groups together for long periods. If the original concept takes off and is successful so you make some money and all the members can come together just to work that's good, but if you're living together bands don't last long.*

But Clive was never ambitious in the conventional sense of the word: *Ken Willard who used to run the Cambridge Folk Festival said to me 'you're the only person I've met who doesn't want to be famous'. I suppose that's true. Depends what I'm into at the time. I don't sit around playing music all the time. I like to play but I don't live for music.*

Photo of COB taken in Ralph's garden in Putney. Genevieve is crouching with Ralph's border collie, Jessie.

As the 70's went on the three main members of COB became involved in other projects. John Bidwell moved to London having met hurdy-

189

gurdy player Jake Walton at the Folk Cottage. John: *In the early 70's I shared flats with Jake Walton. First at Bedford Hill, Balham - just up the road from Wizz and Sandy's place. Then in Tournay Road Fulham. Jake and I would go round to Wizz and Sandy's and work out arrangements of John Burke fiddle tunes that Sandy was learning on banjo. It was during this time that C.O.B. broke up.*

Wizz got involved in it on his return from one of his German tours, and he had an EP to do for 'Village Thing', so we went down to Bristol and put down some tracks with him.

Wizz: *Pete Stanley and I had a good act, for its time. We were trailblazers. Musically, though, it was quite limiting for me. So after four years travelling with Pete I went back to doing solo gigs. I then started working, from about 1969, in Germany during their economic boom, and throughout the '70s played thousands of smoky German bars and I guess that's where my thing really came together.'*

It was 1973, and Wizz was one of a number of UK folk-musicians who played widely on the continent. The Village Thing EP included Wizz's song 'When I leave Berlin', recently covered by Bruce Springsteen. Wizz Jones: *It was around the time I tried writing songs and not just relying on my Alan Tunbridge source. I remember driving down with Bert Jansch in my old VW Beetle to record my song 'Freudian Slip'. We drove back to London in the early morning hours through the pouring rain.*

John Bidwell: *The Lazy Farmer thing continued (with the addition of Don Coging) while Jake and I were living in Fulham, and at that time we toured Germany and made the Lazy Farmer album.*

The album was engineered by Connie Plank who is now better known for his work with Kraftwerk and other German electronic music acts.

190

By the early 70's Ralph McTell, Michael Chapman, Wizz Jones and C.O.B., like other performers at the time, had moved away from playing American folk standards, and made careers based on writing and performing original songs instead. Brenda Wootton's project had evolved into something rather different, however.

In 1970 John the Fish married Carrie, a girl who had been a regular audience member at the Folk Cottage, at the registry office in Truro. Fish: *Brenda at that time was so ambitious she was running ahead of herself. I was finding I was spending more and more time away from Cornwall, and it was more difficult because I'd got married and had a dog. Her sights were higher than mine, but we both went on tour together and we went to the first L'Orient Interceltic Folk Festival* (1971).

This trip to Brittany, together with the Sentinel album 'Pasties and Cream' marked the beginning of the end of Fish and Brenda's musical partnership.

By 1971 Pipers had moved from The Count House to The Western Hotel in Alverton, Penzance on what was then the main road through Cornwall to Land's End. The Pipers' programme (see picture) was packed with visiting artists, and during the summer there were concerts every night. Public interest for some gigs was enough to warrant moving them to the nearby St John's Hall. Fish: *The concert with Diz, Pigsty Hill and Jasper Carrot at St John's Hall was a classic. Brenda and I were in the middle of our set when Dave (of the Pigs), said 'We have a big star wanting to come on'. Out walked Andy (of the Pigs) singing one of my songs, followed by Jasper dressed in one of Brenda's dresses, and they brought the house down...*

It was at The Western Hotel that much of 'Pasties and Cream' was recorded. Critiqued by Cyril Tawney in Folk Review magazine, he describes the album as a miscellany of songs and says: *'Brenda is not an intuitive regional stylist...one is aware of a conscious effort to conjure up 'Cornishness', one of the inevitable results of making the concessions necessary to the pursuit of a...professional folk-singing career'.*

Sue Ellery (top left) with boyfriend Tony Lyons at Fish's wedding. To Brenda's right is Mike Sagar with guitarist Steve Hall and wife Denise.

Decameron (top) with Mike Sagar, Sue and boyfriend Tony (sitting on the ground) at 4, Leskinnick Street. Decameron were a progressive folk-rock act that went on to make four albums.

194

John the Fish responds to the idea that her Cornishness was contrived: *It was also said about David Penhaligon, Tell Man, Jethro and Brenda - but then we all do it. We have our 'telephone voice', the voice we use when addressing a crowd, the voice we use amongst friends - we use whatever voice gets the best effect...*

Pasties and Cream is a populist record and, like 'Pipers' Folk' three years before, broadly representative of songs sung in the in club at the time. As well as Cornish crowd-pleasers like Trelawney and Camborne Hill, thanks to Fish, traces of blues and skiffle are still apparent. However, as Brenda found herself working with different collaborators, so her approach began to change. She also found more nuanced ways to express her 'Cornishness'.

Fish: *Brenda was going off in a different direction. When she found herself in the position of being an ambassador for Cornwall she became more interested in Cornish music and the Cornish language.*

It was songwriter and linguist Richard Gendall that introduced Brenda to her new repertoire. Sue Ellery: *Richard wrote over 400 songs for Brenda. He was a teacher at Helston School who spoke fluent Cornish*

Pipers Folk Club Summer Programme

Western Hotel, Penzance, Cornwall

Residents: BRENDA WOOTTON
JOHN THE FISH
STEVE HALL
MIKE SAGAR

CAR PARK - ALL AGES WELCOME

COFFEE AND LICENSED BAR - 8.0 — 11.15 p.m.

Sat.	May	1	PISCES	At the Club
Sat.	May	8	COME ALL YE	" "
Sat.	May	15	SEAN CANNON	" "
Sat.	May	22	TONY CAPSTICK	" "
Sat.	May	29	SHELAGH MACDONALD	" "
Sat.	June	5	SINGING TRADITION	" "
Sat.	June	12	ALLAN TAYLOR	" "
Sat.	June	19	STRANGE FRUIT	" "
Tues.	June	22	**RALPH MACTELL**, BRENDA WOOTTON, JOHN THE FISH	Concert at ST. JOHN'S HALL
Sat.	June	26	WIZZ JONES	At the Club
Sat.	July	3	GERRY LOCKRAN	" "
Sun.–Tues.	July	4–6	PAUL WEAVING	" "
Weds.–Sat.	July	7–10	DECAMERON	" "
Sun.–Sat.	July	11–17	THE YETTIES	" "
Sun.–Mon.	July	18–19	THE WAYFARERS	" "
Tues.	July	20	**MICHAEL CHAPMAN & BAND,** WAYFARERS, BRENDA & FISH	Concert at ST. JOHN'S HALL
Weds.–Sat.	July	21–24	JON BETMEAD	At the Club
Sun.–Tues.	July	25–27	WHITE ON BLACK	" "
Weds.–Sat.	July	28–31	1812	" "
Sun.–Mon.	Aug.	1–2	JOHNNY COLLINS	" "
Tues.	Aug.	3	**MAGNA CARTA,** JOHNNY COLLINS, BRENDA & FISH	Concert at ST. JOHN'S HALL
Weds.–Sat.	Aug.	4–7	ALEX ATTERSON	At the Club
Sun.–Tues.	Aug.	8–11	MARTIN WYNDHAM-READE	" "
Weds.–Sat.	Aug.	11–14	NOEL MURPHY	" "
Sun.–Mon.	Aug.	15–16	JASPER CARROTT	" "
Tues.	Aug.	17	**DIZ DISLEY, PIGSTY HILL LIGHT ORCHESTRA,** JASPER CARROTT, BRENDA & FISH	Concert at St. JOHN'S HALL
Weds.–Sat.	Aug.	18–21	TIM HART & MADDY PRIOR	At the Club
Sun.–Tues.	Aug.	22–24	PETE RYDER	" "
Weds.–Sat.	Aug.	25–28	JACK HUDSON	" "
Sun.–Mon.	Aug.	29–30	KELSTON ROUNDHILL	" "
Tues.	Aug.	31	**STEEL-EYE SPAN,** BRENDA & FISH	Concert at ST. JOHN'S HALL
Weds.–Sat.	Sept.	1–4	DEREK BRIMSTONE	At the Club

N.B.—The Club will not be open on Concert Nights

SATURDAYS ONLY AFTER THIS DATE (the autumn programme will be out in August)

PRICES: FOR THE CLUB: Members 25p   Non-members 30p
         FOR THE CONCERTS: "   50p   "   60p

TICKETS FOR THE CONCERTS WILL BE AVAILABLE FROM THE ORGANISER; THE CLUB; THE WESTERN HOTEL; and TREMAEN CRAFT MARKET, PENZANCE

TO GET TO THE CLUB: The Western Hotel is on the main A30 road on the Land's End side of Penzance . . . . St. John's Hall is 50 yards further on . . . . .
LARGE CAR PARK BEHIND
       Club Membership - 25p per year from April 1st

Brenda Wootton and John the Fish have a new L.P. out in June, issued on the SENTINEL label (SENS-1006) called "Pasties and Cream"; mainly Cornish material . . . can be ordered from the Club, Mr. Wootton, or Tremaen Craft Market, Penzance . . . will also be on sale throughout West Country music shops

JOHN E. WOOTTON, Coombe Dingle, 4 Leskinnick Street, Penzance, Cornwall

1971 at Pipers Folk

and was a brilliant writer of songs. He would write some in Cornish and some in English, but they were all about Cornwall.

As a young man in his twenties Richard Gendall had struck up a friendship with one of the first Bards of the Cornish Gorsedd and founders of the Old Cornwall society: Robert Morton Nance. Richard: *In 1938 Morton Nance did a Cornish into English dictionary. It's not a bad dictionary. Then he did an English into Cornish which came out in 1952, which I prepared for him. I took his 1938 dictionary and reversed it. He was living at Carbis Bay at the time.*

I was born in 1924. I was a student at Leeds University studying languages. In my teens I'd been given a copy of his dictionary by my parents as a Christmas present and I was longing to find out all I could about Cornish. When I came back from the war and went to University I got into touch with him, and we had a loose friendship and exchanged letters and so on.

Early in 1972 Brenda had been approached by the Celtic League to represent Cornwall at a festival: *Brenda was asked to go to the Killarney Pan Celtic Festival in Ireland, and she had to sing a song in the Cornish language. I gave her the English-Cornish folk song 'Tryphena Trenerry' and another one. There weren't any songs in the Cornish language then so I supplied her with one of my own which passes as folk music in Cornish.*

She went across and was well received, and that sparked off an interest in music relating to Cornwall and eventually to the Cornish language.

She didn't know that much about it at first. She didn't really know what was Cornish and what wasn't, so I sent her stuff from Baring-Gould and other sources - for example 'Soldier on the Battlefield' and 'Jan Knuckey'.

I gave her lots of stuff that she hadn't heard of. We used to spend evenings going through them, at Leskinnick and at her place in Penzance near the harbour, and she used to come to my place near Camborne.

Brenda eating a pasty at the Killarney Pan Celtic Festival, 1972 with guitarist Steve Hall (centre) and Cousin Malc (right)

Sue Ellery (flip-flops), Ella Knight (centre) her dog Supertool and Jonathan March, Dave Bell and Geoff March of Decameron, Norwich Folk Festival 1973. Photo Sue Ellery.

We would spend hours together with a guitarist learning them by rote. She prided herself on not being a trained musician. She tended to make mistakes; to mislearn things. And once she'd learnt a mistake it was hopeless and hard to get it right again! But she was a great performer and she took masses of my stuff.

Sue Ellery: *The relationship Brenda developed with Richard was vitally important to her career as a singer. When she became very famous and well-known on the continent she would be away for 2 or 3 months at a time, singing every night. But she would get an idea in her head about a song that she wanted, and she would phone him and say 'I need a song about the Merry Maidens' or 'I need a song about this or that Cornish Legend', and within 48 hours he would have written it and sent it to her, and it would be brilliant.So, for example, when Brenda went to Australia she asked Dick to write a song about 'The Mystery' which was the ship that took the first miners to Australia.*

Richard *I'd written a little music but Brenda spurred me on and I wrote more and more and more. As long as she was able to take them I was able to compose them.*

Richard also taught Brenda to speak a limited amount of Cornish: *Brenda wasn't very good at Cornish. She would learn it parrot-fashion but never told anyone that she didn't really understand it. But she was such a good performer and she'd stand up on the stage and bold as brass she'd sing anything. She presented herself so well with everyone hanging on her every word that no-one challenged her or thought to ask her where things came from...*

Sue: *Part of the problem with learning Cornish is that you don't know which version you should be learning. One version assumes that the language as it died out 200 years ago should be unchanged, the other assumes that it would have developed in the intervening years. So you get all this scholastic argument going on.*

Richard distinguishes between modern and medieval Cornish: *All Cornish up to about 1600 was based on religious drama, like the Ordinalia and Mystery Plays. And you can't really base a revival of a language on religious drama. When you get to 1660 there are one or two writers who have nothing at all to do with the church. They were writing the language as they knew it and it looks completely different.*

That's where modern Cornish comes in. When you get to 1700 the principle writer was called John Boson - and that's how the language looked when it was used by ordinary people just before it died out.

Richard contributed songs to many of Brenda's albums after 1971, but his involvement was greatest in the Sentinel LP 'Crowdy Crawn' which was released in 1973, its title referring to a type of Cornish drum.

The record is a pioneering attempt to make the language more accessible, and it succeeds by emphasizing its musicality. After the needle drops onto the vinyl, we hear Richard speaking in a gently lilting Cornish. The inner sleeve provides an English translation:

Crowdy Crawn (1973). Cover designed by Brenda Wootton's brother Peter Ellery. The inner sleeve contains lyrics and prose in English and Cornish.

Well now friends and God bless you all.
Stay with us a little while.
We have here a Cornish sampler
And so mates – be of good cheer.
Brenda m'dear, if you are quite ready
Let's tip out the Crowdy Crawn
and everybody standby

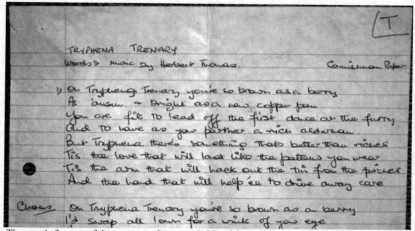

The words for one of the songs on the second side of Crowdy Crawn, as copied out by Brenda from its original source in the Cornishman paper. Herbert Thomas, who wrote 'Pasties and Cream' as well as 'Tryphena Trenary', was editor of the newspaper at the turn of the century.

The rest of the record is a bricolage of poems and songs in both English and Cornish, with many of the songs featuring a similar spoken introduction. Richard Gendall plays guitar on the record: *I didn't play music in public. I played guitar for my own accompaniment. Irene and Job Morris also produced a record called 'Children Singing' (1976) and I played guitar on that and on 'Crowdy Crawn' but I don't pride myself on being a super guitarist. I never played in the clubs.*

In truth there is n't much Cornish language folk music. There is just one song with music and words and even that's slightly doubtful. 'Pela era why moaz' or 'Delyo Syvy' is a Cornish version of 'Where are you going to my pretty maid'. There is a tune that goes to it but no-one is sure if it's the right tune or not. It's very sketchy.

There is a certain amount of English language Cornish folk music. Even then there is not a vast quantity and all the genuine stuff is in collections published by Sabine Baring-Gould and Ralph Dunstan. There is the odd one or two in Cecil Sharp house (EFDSS HQ) that I picked up that hadn't appeared anywhere else.

You can't write genuine folk music because it's developed over a number of years. You can only take it and adapt it or whatever. My

201

music is based on themes that are common to the whole of Britain. I was strongly influenced by Welsh, Irish and Scottish music.

Sue: *Brenda's love of Cornwall was what she carried with her and Richard's music was the vehicle that enabled her to pass that on to everybody. When the flow of Richard's songs dried up she didn't say that much about it because she had so many by that time. She had songs that she'd never got round to performing because each one she would have to spend a long time on to make sure that she'd perfected it before she brought it out in public. And some never did get brought out in public.*

Mike Sagar played guitar on Piper's Folk and other recordings made by Brenda in the 70's: *'Crowdy Crawn' is the first record I know that has the Cornish language on it. I played a couple of tracks on that. I played on 'Morvah Fair' which were songs we just picked up. Richard was more precise in his guitar playing, he played in a classical style with nylon strings. He wanted to make it sound authentic, but he was also interested in writing new stuff.*

Mike recalls Brenda on stage at that time: *Brenda would explain what the songs were about. She would talk about Cornwall, her family, the local ice-cream shop, whatever. She was extremely good at telling stories. There's a song called 'Tamar' that she did, which is a sad and beautiful song. She would introduce it by talking about the Vikings who fought with the Cornish in the Tamar Valley, and telling the whole elaborate back-story.*

I went with her as an accompanist to the Isle of Wight. We did a festival which was amazing. She walked onto the main stage - the fat lady - and England, unlike France, is quite intolerant of people's shapes, so they all tittered. And I could see she was thinking 'I'm going to sort this lot out'. So she sang some of her most challenging songs at the beginning, and they immediately started to take her seriously. And at the end they were up stamping and clapping and in the palm of her hand. She had this incredible sense of what an audience was and how to work it.

I also remember the Cambridge Folk Festival. I remember meeting a lot of Cornish people there. Because our folk scene was so strong and most of the people on the bill we knew because they had played at our clubs. It was very villagey and nice to begin with.

Brenda Wootton, with Dick Gendall's support, was instrumental in popularising the Cornish revival, and in creating the image of Cornwall that we have now. Mike Sagar: *At primary school we did Scottish dancing and sang nationalist songs like 'Rule Britannia', but nothing folky and certainly nothing Cornish. The teachers wanted to teach us Latin and that sort of thing, but our local culture was completely neglected.*

Brenda at the Cambridge Folk Festival mid 70s

Nobody had recorded in Cornish before or explored the tradition. And Brenda took this music all around the world, in Cornish colonies in Canada and Australia and other Celtic Nations.

In 1973 Brenda met guitarist and singer Robert Bartlett. The sleeve-notes to 'No song to sing', the LP they made together in 1974, describes their meeting: *'Friends for several years, they came together musically while on holiday at the Northumberland home of Michael Chapman. At Michael's insistence, they got together - with virtually no song to sing - for a concert at the Greenland Hotel'.*

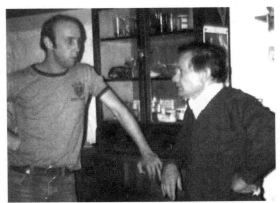

Guitarist Robert Barlett (left) and Richard Gendall (right) meeting for a practice at Richard's house c1973.

Sue Ellery: *By the time they met, Brenda was fairly well established and had done a few tours around the country. She'd have also done things like the Killarney Pan Celtic Festival, Cambridge Folk Festival, Trowbridge Village Pump Festival, Towersey Festival in Oxfordshire.*

Despite Brenda's burgeoning reputation, they agreed to perform as equal partners under the name 'Crowdy Crawn'. Their LP was recorded in Cornwall, and, released by Sentinel, it includes three Richard Gendall songs, two of which were sung by Brenda in Cornish. It also includes a traditional blues song, and a cover of 'Forever Young' by Bob Dylan. The title track is particularly poignant, written as it was by mutual friend Michael Chapman, who had recently appeared on The Old Grey Whistle test TV show, having completed his third album on EMI.

At the time Brenda was busy. Sue: *Brenda was running Tremaen's Craft Market, as well as running the folk club and The Choughs and working in the pottery. Her brother Peter had set up the market in the middle of Penzance behind Humphrey Davy Statue in the bottom part of Lloyds Bank. It was a vehicle for Tremaen pottery but the ethos was that he would only be selling Cornish-made craft products - principally pottery.*

The Tremaen Pottery in a newspaper cutting from 1972, days before a visit by Princess Anne. Brenda who is seen here with her father, Angus and brother, Peter, would become a full-time singer two years later.

Then early in 1974 Brenda called me into the shop to say that she wanted to turn professional as a singer with Robert, and would I take over as manager of the shop. I was struggling as I had only had supply teaching jobs. I remember being quite choked up to think that mother thought I could do it. So I took over the shop and she and Robert took off to Brittany.

They had a very intense musical relationship. For both of them it was very exciting. It was like all of a sudden things were happening. She formed many friendships in France. There was a woman called Gwenn Le Goarnig. Her family had a chateau on the West coast of France called Kerltag, and they regarded themselves as the royal family of Brittany. She organised some festivals.

Three albums were produced as a result of the Kerltag festivals in '72, '73 and '74: *The records caused no end of trouble as Gwenn's idea of producing an album was to record everybody at the festival, bring it out, and forget to tell everyone who was on the album!*

Kerltag 1973. Brenda draped with a St Piran flag practicing with Dik Cadbury (Decameron) and Rene Vermeer, before (below) appearing on stage. Photo Sue Ellery.

Brenda must have had a lot of bookings then. She brought out an album in France called 'Pamplemousse'. Barclay Records, which brought out Pamplemousse also brought out a single of 'Mordonnow', by Richard Gendall (see photo).

Sue helped keep the family business going without Brenda: *By the mid 70's we had every local studio pottery represented in the shop. The big three in Newlyn at that time were Tremaen, Troika and Celtic pottery.*

When mother was involved in the pottery it was a very happy little work place in a fishloft upstairs in the corner of Newlyn Harbour. Peter was the designer. He used Cot Valley boulders to make gorgeously rounded organic shapes. He would find a stone he liked the shape of, and make a cast of it in plaster of Paris. You'd roll out the clay like pastry, then lay it inside the mould.

The pendants were Brenda's idea. She was responsible for packing and unpacking the kilns and overseeing the production. When she started the folk club we made little clay pendants of Brenda and Fish. A little fat Brenda, and Fish with his beard and a guitar! They'd have been taken to festivals and been sold at the club.

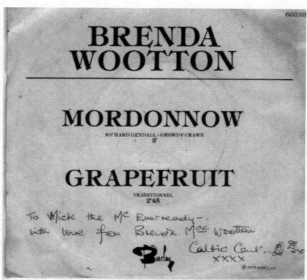

'To Mick the McEver-ready with love from Brenda MacWootton'. Collection Mic McCreadie

One of Brenda's clay pendant designs

Brenda made two more albums with Robert Bartlett: 'Starry Gazey Pie' and 'Tin in the Stream'. The former record contains no traces of American folk, unlike 'No Song to Sing', and is a charming collection of intimately sung traditional tunes, in which Brenda and Robert share vocals.

Then, shortly after the Norwich Folk Festival in 1975 Brenda and Robert went their separate ways. Sue: *Alex Atterson was one of the prime movers in the Norwich Folk Festival, so we used to go every year. It was held at the University of East Anglia. The football match played there in '74 is the stuff of legend. Brenda was in goal (see photo). It's the only game of football she played in her life! Chapman is in there looking cool in a denim shirt.*

Norwich sticks in my mind probably because of the Brenda-Robert thing. Their musical career was so impressive and so fiery. It was quite dramatic.

At the second Norwich Festival in '75 Robert met my cousin Diane and the two fell in love. It was around this time there were huge rows between him and Brenda. When they finally split up they were away on tour in Scotland...

Singer-songwriter Mike Silver became Brenda's new accompanist, and in 1975 they went on a tour of continental Europe. Mike's career had taken some spectacular twists and turns in the four years since forming Daylight with Chrissy Quayle. This included a prestigious record deal and solo tour of America: *During Christmas 1971. I was in Cornwall. I took some LSD and had a nightmare trip. It was like I was trapped in my own body. It was terrifying.*

Brenda, wearing her cloak whilst acting as goalkeeper, during a football match at the Norwich Folk Festival 1974, held on the campus of UEA.

I didn't dare tell my parents, so I hung out in Cornwall. But I told Brenda because she was always kind to me. Then I was sitting in her kitchen one day having some toast, and she said: 'When are you going home to see your Mum and Dad? You should you know. Here's £25' and she gave me the money for the journey.

Once recovered, Mike returned to London, met Elton John and was signed to his new label: *I was the second or third artist to be signed to Rocket Records. Del Newman who wrote the arrangements on 'Goodbye Yellow Brick Road' got me the deal. He said 'If you put a demo together I'll take it to Rocket'. The five directors Elton John, Bernie*

209

Taupin (lyricist), Gus Dudgeon (producer), John Reid (manager - and Queen's manager) and Steve Brown (engineer) all loved it. I was completely star-struck by the whole thing. I was sat across the table from those five guys and one of them said 'you are going to be very rich and very famous', and when you're 27 and people like that say that to you, you believe them.

The Troubadour was a famous folk club in Earls Court., here used as the sleeve image for Mike Silver's album on Rocket Records. Mike was a regular visitor to the Troubadour, and he befriended Del Newman there.

The subsequent tour, in 1973, included some of the most famous music venues in the USA: venues which Michael Chapman had missed out on the previous year. However there were signs that Mike Silver had fallen out of favour: *They sent me to the States to become famous overnight. But I wasn't ready. I did three nights at The Troubadour in Los Angeles. And Elton John came over to see the first night, and he stared at me from the front row not applauding, just looking very bored. Then I went to New York and played 6 nights at Max's Kansas City. The last gig was six nights with Peter Yarrow (Peter, Paul and Mary) at The Cellar Door Washington. When I came back to England, Rocket stopped answering my calls and rescinded my contract.*

Then I went to Amsterdam in 1974 and was living on a boat when I heard that Brenda was in need of a guitar player so I rang her up and said 'I'll give you six months'.

She and John came to Holland and spent a weekend in Amsterdam. We all went back to Cornwall in their car a few days later. We spent a week or so rehearsing at Brenda's, did a couple of warm-up gigs in the UK, then travelled to Europe. We played the songs she'd been doing with Rob Bartlett. A lot of songs about Cornwall and some songs by Richard Gendall.

There was TV producer in France that really liked what she did. So part of our tour involved going to France to do a thing on French TV.

Brenda chats with Ted Heath in a Beer Cellar in Brussels (1975). Ted Heath had recently had four years as Prime Minister. Mike Silver is in the background.

So we went to the TV studios and, like a true pro, Brenda sang like an angel, but then started saying that she was feeling sick and went to bed early. When I checked in on her at about 9 o'clock she was awake but she didn't recognise me. She was delirious and looked awful. I got the agent to call a doctor who spoke perfect English: 'She s got a very bad infection. I've given her a big shot of antibiotics. If you hadn't have called me she would have died within 4 hours'.

211

In fact Brenda took the TV appearance in her stride. There was a full orchestra there, so I was pretty much surplus to requirements. It was broadcast live and I could only just hear what I was playing.

That year we also did a British TV series called 'Sweet Somerset'. It was made in HTV in Bristol. She was spending a lot of time away from home during this period and John and Sue were keeping Piper's going whilst she was away.

Late in 1974 Pipers moved from The Western Hotel to The London Inn nearer the centre of Penzance, then a couple of years later to The Meadery at Gulval. A photograph shows Brenda returning as a special guest, wearing a floral dress and silver brooch. Al Fenn previously of Decameron had taken over from Mike Silver as her regular accompanist. Sue: *Brenda had two brooches, both silver with three amethyst stones. The design is a Celtic triskel, a Breton symbol similar to the Isle of Man's three legs. She had a matching ring with a single stone, and wore the brooch at every concert for years - and silver rings on every finger and thumbs sometimes. And that grew over time as people gave her rings, or made rings especially for her. When she had publicity photos done she would show her hands and show the rings.*

The dress, with its lace collar, was made by Brenda herself: *Brenda made all her own dresses. She had notebooks in which she put her own designs. I can remember many occasions when we'd be shopping and she would find some fabric. She would go for flowing polyesters that would hang well on stage, but which wouldn't crease when shoved into a suitcase. She could work out how much material she needed. She knew that if she got 5 yards of material it could be gathered so it would hang nicely.*

She was always very conscious of her shape. After she gave birth to me she developed this huge belly, but wearing full length dresses was a way of drawing people's eyes away from that.

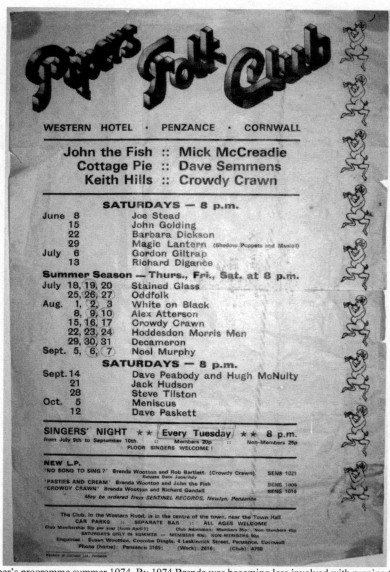

Piper's Folk Club

WESTERN HOTEL · PENZANCE · CORNWALL

John the Fish :: Mick McCreadie
Cottage Pie :: Dave Semmens
Keith Hills :: Crowdy Crawn

SATURDAYS — 8 p.m.

June 8	Joe Stead
15	John Golding
22	Barbara Dickson
29	Magic Lantern (Shadow Puppets and Music)
July 6	Gordon Giltrap
13	Richard Digance

Summer Season — Thurs., Fri., Sat. at 8 p.m.

July 18, 19, 20	Stained Glass
25, 26, 27	Oddfolk
Aug. 1, 2, 3	White on Black
8, 9, 10	Alex Atterson
15, 16, 17	Crowdy Crawn
22, 23, 24	Hoddesdon Morris Men
29, 30, 31	Decameron
Sept. 5, 6, 7	Noel Murphy

SATURDAYS — 8 p.m.

Sept. 14	Dave Peabody and Hugh McNulty
21	Jack Hudson
28	Steve Tilston
Oct. 5	Meniscus
12	Dave Paskett

SINGERS' NIGHT ★★ Every Tuesday ★★ 8 p.m.

from July 9th to September 10th. :: Members 20p :: Non-Members 25p
FLOOR SINGERS WELCOME !

NEW L.P.

'NO SONG TO SING ?' Brenda Wootton and Rob Bartlett. (Crowdy Crawn).   SENS 1021
Release Date June/July
'PASTIES AND CREAM' Brenda Wootton and John the Fish   SENS 1005
'CROWDY CRAWN' Brenda Wootton and Richard Gendall   SENS 1016
May be ordered from SENTINEL RECORDS, Newlyn Penzance

The Club, in the Western Hotel, is in the centre of the town, near the Town Hall
CAR PARKS :: SEPARATE BAR :: ALL AGES WELCOME
Club Membership 30p per year (from April 1)   Club Admission: Members 35p   Non-Members 45p
SATURDAYS ONLY IN SUMMER — MEMBERS 50p; NON-MEMBERS 50p
Enquiries :: Susan Wootton, Coombe Dingle, 4 Leskinnick Street, Penzance, Cornwall
Phone (home): Penzance 3165;   (Work): 2616;   (Club): 4798

Piper's programme summer 1974. By 1974 Brenda was becoming less involved with running the club.

213

Late 70's. Brenda returning to Pipers, the club she started in 1967, as a special guest at The Meadery, Gulval. The guitarist in the photo is Al Fenn, ex-Decameron.

In a photograph from earlier in the 70's, Brenda can be seen sitting out-side, making a dress out of Cornish tartan: *The tartan dress would have been for performances. It was very uncomfortable. Very itchy. It was wool! The sort of thing you'd make a coat out of really. I don't remember her wearing it a lot.*

The photo in question was taken at 'The Stack': Brenda and John's country retreat outside Penzance, bought earlier in the 70's. Sue: *When Brenda was still running Tremaen Craft Market she told her solicitor that she was on the look out for a bolt-hole. The house in Leskinnick Street was always full of people and she wanted somewhere to escape to. One day he contacted her and said 'There is an old chalet up on the moors coming up for sale'. It had been on the beach in Marazion and was moved to a quarry near Ding Dong Mine. She fell in love with it and sent a cheque for £1500 to the guy that owned it. It was an old wooden shack, but it had a front room with a beautiful panoramic win-dow looking across to Mulfra, with a back bedroom and a little kitchenette .*

Mike Sagar: *The Stack was more private. It wasn't a case of 'everyone come back to my place', you had to be invited there. By the early eight-ies she decided she wanted to live up there. She was getting older, and even her energy ran out in the end.*

'Up The Stack': Brenda making a Cornish tartan dress for the Killarney Festival in 1972. Photo Sue Ellery.

Brenda and Martin Carthy at The Stack. Martin was a solo performer for many years, and also a member of Steeleye Span.

1977 was a special year for Brenda Wootton, marked as it was by two events of great personal significance. At the age of 49 she became a grandmother, when Sue gave birth to her first son, Davy. Sue: *When mother became a grandmother for the first time she asked Richard for the appropriate Cornish word. Richard said the term would be 'Damawyn' which means 'fair dame'. It's the name of the matriarch, the oldest woman in the family. So she was never 'Granny', she was 'Damawyn'.*

Then, in September Brenda was made a bard in recognition of her services to Cornish culture, and took the bardic name 'Gwylan Gwavas', Cornish for Seagull of Newlyn. Sue: *She was so proud of being made a bard of the Cornish Gorsedd. She was bursting with pride at the honour.*

The Cornishman paper's report ran as follows: *There was special applause for the last to be initiated, folk singer Brenda Wootton...She was thrilled by the occasion: 'I was very moved by the ceremony. It was so dignified. Everything was perfect'...When Mrs Wootton returned to Penzance there was a great welcome from 270 at the Piper's Folk Club.*

The club could certainly still pull large audiences, but Mrs Wootton was not the only show in town. In what is a startling and almost implausible juxtaposition, the paper that week featured both Brenda in her bardic robes, and on the front page, a blond Sid Vicious posing in Chapel Street in Penzance. The Sex Pistols, potent symbols of a different, more nihilistic cultural world, had just played at The Garden.

Now with booking agents in Germany, Belgium and France, Brenda was actually spending more time abroad than she did in Cornwall, usually travelling on the ferry between Plymouth and Roscoff in Britanny.

Sue: *She was a regular on the car-ferry. She got to know some of the boatmen quite well. Father didn't usually go with her. More often than not it would be just her and the guitarist - and later on a roadie.*

Brenda , with her grandsons, proudly wearing her bardic robes at a Gorsedd ceremony in the early 80's.

Brenda's diaries in the late 70's are packed with bookings, and each month she spent a least a week abroad. In 1979, for example, she went to France and Belgium, each on three separate occasions, performing at the Theatre de la Ville in Paris on one of the trips (see photo).

Accompanied by guitarist Dave Penhale, that same year she also went to Germany four times *and* managed a tour of Australia and the Isle of Man.

Sue: *Her main career was France, Holland, Belgium and Germany. She would do a circuit of Western Europe. She sang in Australia several times, especially in South Australia where there is a big Cornish contingent from miners' 19th century families.*

Her popularity in France, especially following performances on TV and in several of the large theatres in Paris, is attested to by the extensive press coverage she received in papers as diverse as Le Figaro, Le Monde and Elle. But it wasn't all plain sailing. In 1976, in an interview for the Melody Maker, Brenda describes moving away from her identity as a folk singer: *'You're called a folk singer because you work the only scene available to you and that's the folk scene'.* She also describes some inner conflict: *'I'm a middle-aged woman with a family, and*

217

sometimes I ache and I yearn to be home, but there's no way I could give this up'...'I like the life of a housewife. I am a good housewife and a good cook, but my husband's a good man and he's made many sacrifices to let me do this. This is what I was born to do'.

Letters to Sue and John from Paris reveal even more ambivalence. Sue: *She used to get very tired, and sometimes quite depressed. Her and Father used to have rows, but he very much supported her. He was her rock. Eventually he gave up his job, because Brenda had become the main breadwinner and so he realised it was better for him to just support her in her music.*

In the ensuing years, Brenda recorded five more albums. Then, two decades after Clive, Wizz and Ralph performed in Paris as buskers, in 1984 she had a series of six sell-out shows at the historic Bobino Theatre, supported by Camborne Town Band and a trio of accompanists including guitarist Chris Newman. The event was recorded for posterity by engineer John Knight.

In fact a number of other musicians popular in Cornwall, like Wizz Jones and Lazy Farmer, Mike Silver, Mick Bennett and Pete Berryman, found work performing on the continent during the 70's.

Brenda Wootton , with David Penhale in Paris, 1979. The poster is for a concert at The Theatre de la Ville

218

Carved from Cornish Elm by her grandson, Davy, the grave of Brenda Wootton ('Gwylan Gwavas') and husband John ('Mr Woottie') in Paul cemetery (2012). Brenda died in 1994, and John two years later.

John the Fish was also amongst them: *Brenda and I decided we were going to go in different directions. So I started working with Alex Atterson who had previously gone abroad with John Pearse, who was a wizard guitarist who brought out guitar-playing books. He had contacts in Holland and Germany and he asked me to go out there on tour with him.*

Fish released a solo album in 1975. It includes the FJB's 'A leaf must fall' by Clive Palmer and songs by David Dearlove, Alan Tunbridge and Michael Chapman. *Ceolacanth was recorded in Wales. Jo Stead had this record company and asked me to make the record. I went with Alex (Atterson) and recorded it up there...*

Chapter 13: Old Clubs & New Festivals

The Cornwall Folk Festival, which started in Wadebridge in 1973, evolved out of festivals that had been held in Falmouth since 1969. It included dance displays, craft workshops and Punch and Judy as well as music.

Cornwall Folk Festival, 1975. Photo and additional info courtesy Roger Hancock.

John The Fish: *There were at least three Falmouth Folk Festivals, backed by the EFDSS, prior to the Cornwall Folk Festival in Wadebridge (also, originally backed by EFDSS). They were held in venues in the town, but as the festival grew in 1972 they hired a marquee. Unfortunately that year they were greeted with gale-force winds and*

*torrential rain. The marquee blew away and the festival was a wash-
out. The committee lost heart and, no doubt, money.*

The St Ives Festival, also still going strong, grew out of the many gigs
Martin Val Baker organised during the 70's. In 1972 he had acted as
roadie to Bob Devereux's 'Bocuvm', now going under the name
'Mask', as they undertook a national tour. On returning he organised
more concerts, often booking performers that had appeared in the
Cornish clubs in the 60's. This included Mick Bennett and Tim Wellard
as part of 'Scarlet Runner'. Martin: *'Scarlet Runner' were probably the
best of the creative musicians around in West Cornwall in the mid-
seventies, and carried on in another equally good incarnation as a duo,
'Crooks and Nannies'.*

In 1976 Martin acted as manager to Clive Palmer and Bob Devereux
who had started working together after Clive had returned to live in
Cornwall: *Bob and Clive's set would include about 75% working
together and then solo pieces by each of them, practically all of the
words would be original material. Later we went to a proper recording
studio and recorded 'Suns and Moons' a cassette that is now something
of a collector's item and was much later released as a C.D. Years afterwards a track from this C.D. was chosen by Billy Connolly (an old
friend of Clive's from Edinburgh in the sixties) as one of his 'Desert
Island Discs'.* MVB memoirs

Martin's original idea had been to organise a folk festival in St Ives,
centred on The Guildhall, but the concept was expanded so that, in
1978, it became a full-blown multimedia arts festival. Thanks largely to
Bernard Leach's world-renowned pottery, St Ives had been central to
the rebirth of handicraft in the 20th century: *The first two-week St Ives
September Festival was launched with Robert Etherington as the paid
coordinator, myself as the booker of a three day folk section, the painter
Patrick Hughes (and later Bob Devereux) booking the poets, and a host
of enthusiastic others looking after other sections of the arts.*

In fact most of the festivals accommodated a wider range of activities
than the folk clubs had. Folk dancing and craft-making were on the
same spectrum as the music: part of a hippy sensibility that favoured the
hand-made and personal over the mass-produced. John the Fish became
known for making clogs that were suitable for dancing in. Fish: *Craft
stalls were a big part of all the festivals. I was into leather-craft at the*

221

time: making belts, bags, hats, pouches, hair slides etc. Later, when I got into clog dancing, I made and sold clogs, and in fact Roger Taylor from Queen came and bought some from me. They were based on North Country clogs, rather than Scandinavian clogs, and were made for dancing.

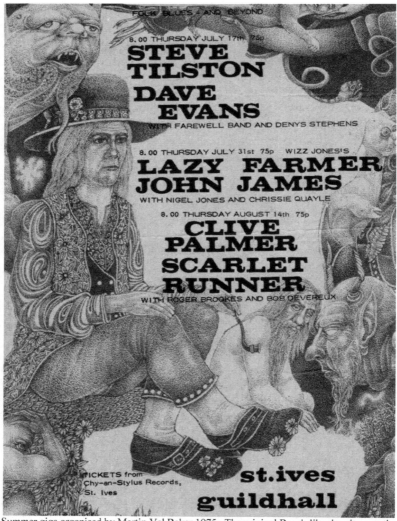

Summer gigs organised by Martin Val Baker 1975. The original Bosch-like drawings on the posters were by Terry Pascoe, one of Martin's art school friends. Lazy Farmer included John Bidwell and Jake Walton (ex Folk Cottage), Scarlet Runner included Mick Bennett and Tim Wellard (ex Stockroom Five).

L to R Mic McCreadie, his then girlfriend Yvonne, Fish and his wife Carrie and dog, Cain at Polgooth Country Fayre. Pinned to the vertical board are Fish's hand-made leather belts and hair-slides. On the table are hats, and other leatherware.

The generation that had formed the membership of CND as beatniks, were now pioneering environmental consciousness, vegetarianism and the Green movement. Polgooth Country Fayre was a festival that ran for three years from 1977, and it epitomised the spirit of the times. Fish was a stall-holder there, and Bob Butler one of the main organisers. Bob: *In the late 1960's and the 1970's Cornwall was a haven for those of us who shared a vision of an alternative lifestyle. There were a lot of small-holdings, and people exploring self-sufficiency, a number of wholefood shops (Goodness Gracious in St Austell, The Granary in Truro), the beginnings of alternative therapies/medicines, a couple of alternative bookshops, lots of craftspeople, and so on.*

There was a high concentration of this activity in the mid-Cornwall area around Mevagissey and St Austell, and a whole community living in and around Heligan Woods. Musicians Mick Bennett and Pete Berryman lived in Heligan at various times and Ralph McTell bought a house close by in London Apprentice. Polgooth Fayre was very much rooted in this community and we tried to harness all these strands to make a statement about viable alternative lifestyles.

223

Wizz Jones, Mick Bennett and Clive Palmer play an impromptu set at Polgooth Fayre (1979?).
Photo: Mic McCreadie

After the Fayre in 1979, when veterans of the 60's folk scene like Wizz
Jones, Robin Williamson (ISB) and Clive Palmer shared the stage with
local new wave acts like Brainiac Five, it moved east to the Eliot estate
in St Germans. Bob: *I was determined to refine the idea of a multi-
disciplined arts festival and so started to look for a site for another
festival in 1981. I heard a whisper about a crazy 'hippy' Lord who lived
in St Germans. Apparently he had worked for The Beatles in his youth
and had later inherited a rather grand pile and was, by all accounts,
well worth talking to. So I called up his Estate Manager and made an
appointment to meet with the gentleman in question: Lord Peregrine
Eliot. This was a memorable meeting. Peregrine turned up in jeans and
a very moth-eaten jumper, put his feet up on his antique desk, rolled a
joint and, basically, said 'Yes, let's do it'.*

Renamed Elephant Fayre, the festival enjoyed seven more colourful
years, performances by top bands like The Cure, and crowds of over
30,000, until the idealism of the original 70's festival movement was
finally shattered by the so-called 'Peace Convoy'.

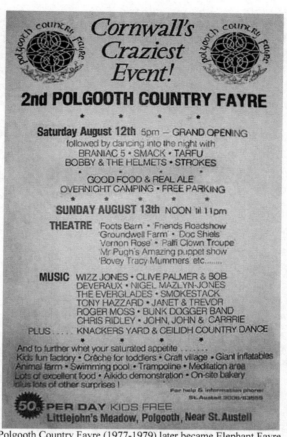

Polgooth Country Fayre (1977-1979) later became Elephant Fayre.

Other Cornish festivals, like Skinner's Bottom Folk Festival, came and went in the 70's and 80's but one other, also started in 1978, has survived through to the present day.

Several years younger than the original Folk Cottage musicians, in the early 70's Merv Davey temporarily moved from his native Cornwall to London. Then, in 1975, he returned to live in Falmouth: *By '75 the folk scene in Cornwall had become polarised between contemporary and trad folk, so there were some folk clubs that would follow the Steeleye Span example and 'rock things up', but there were others that would not even allow a guitar in.*

Even the more traditional clubs, like that in Bodmin, tended to celebrate the English folk tradition, rather than explore a more specific Cornish repertoire: *The folk scene and Cornish tradition were still quite separate. Even at Fal Folk there was very little Cornish stuff sung, though they were sympathetic to it possibly due to the influence of two of the organisers, who were active members of Mebyon Kernow.*

I actually learnt Cornish songs not from the folk clubs but by going to the Sailor's Arms pub (Newquay). I had to be quite mature before I recognised pub-singing as folk. To me folk was a guitar and singing Wizz Jones-type stuff.

Merv wrote the Cornish song book 'Hengan', which came out in 1983, as part of an undertaking to put this right: *I collected my very first song in 1975. It was a version of Little Lize. 'Hengan' was a mixture of archival research and living tradition. In Plymouth Museum there were copies of Baring-Gould's manuscripts and there were a lot of songs and notes of songs that hadn't been published before. So I published things that hadn't made it into the Dunstan or Gundry books.*

I was part of the Cornish movement, and people I knew would sing in clubs and festivals, and there was need for an extended repertoire to sing in Cornish. It was a book for us all to use to sing and add to that repertoire.

It was the festivals, rather than the folk clubs, that acted as the true catalyst for this change: *The Celtic Festival scene erupted at the beginning of the 70's and had a big impact. The two that kicked it off were the Festival Interceltique in L'Orient, Brittany, and the Killarney Pan Celtic Festival in Ireland.*

The Celtic music was very different to what was played in the Mitchell Folk Cottage. What happened was that Cornish trad music started to be interpreted in a Celtic way. From about 1976 they needed people to sing in Cornish at Celtic events in Cornwall. The Penventon Hotel hosted 2 or 3 concerts, and also hosted the Celtic Congress. We entered the Pan Celtic competition in 1978. We went along with Brenda Wootton at the same time, and won the singing festival there in Killarney.

Kemysk from Cornwall, who won a Celtic Group singing award during Pan Celtic Week in Killarney. (MacMonagle)

Kemysk 1978 Formed at Fal Folk club, taking their name from the Cornish word for 'mixture'. Other Cornish folk groups were formed at the end of the 70s, including 'Bucca', whose members were Merv Davey's younger brothers.

Brenda encouraged us and helped us along and would have said 'you need to go and speak to Dick'. Dick Gendall gave us the song that we won with. It was 'The Mystery'. He wrote it, sung it for us and taught it to us. He used to have a caravan in a field surrounded by small trees. I remember going to see him there, him writing the song out for us and playing it on his guitar.

Then we hired a coach and off we went. We were stunned by what we found at Killarney. Celtique L'Orient and Killarney Pan Celtic very much encouraged us to set up a festival in Cornwall.

That festival, in Perranporth, became known as Lowender Peran, and Brenda Wootton's husband John was the first chairman of the committee. Merv: *The festivals became more important. They were certainly important to me. If I'd sang in Cornish at a folk club there'd be an audience of 20 people, and 15 would immediately go to sleep!! The first time we went to L'Orient we had an audience of 7000!*

Lowender Peran is a folk festival in anthropological terms but people don't see it as a folk festival, they see it as a Celtic festival. We have brass bands, bagpipes and dancers - none of which you'd see in a folk club.

Encouraged by contact with musicians from other Celtic nations, Merv started researching into the Cornish bagpipes: *I've always been interested in bagpipes - but in the context of the Celtic festival you have an audience, a reference group and people to teach you. We had a Cornish bagpipes project, myself and Will Coleman and a couple of others, and we got some sets made and we can now play them.*

After C.O.B. split up Clive Palmer spent a year on a full-time musical instrument technology course at Merton College, before then moving back to Cornwall. He started playing a set of self-made Northumbrian smallpipes (like bagpipes) in some of the clubs locally, including 'Pipers'. Clive: *You have to make them all from scratch. Find the reeds, and make the pipes on a lathe. The hippy generation were always making things.*

It is Clive who is now credited as creating, in 1978, the first modern pair of Cornish bagpipes, which had last been played in the 16th Century. Merv: *I commissioned Clive. They were modelled on the Cornish pipes on the bench end in Davidstow Church, and they worked after a fashion, but were a bit quiet and not really loud enough for dancing in the way described in the medieval texts...*

Merv Davey now plays bagpipes regularly at the Cornish Gorseth, and uses them to lead processions on St Piran's day. This includes a crowd a thousand strong that visits St Piran's Oratory on Perranporth beach on the Sunday closest to March 5th.

In 1980 Merv and his family, together with Brenda Wootton, became involved in staging Cornish musical drama. Sue: *Richard Gendall wrote a couple of major sagas. Merv and his family performed in one of them. Called 'Anne Jeffery and the Little People,' it's about a healer who is accused of witchcraft. She is imprisoned but she thrives in prison, because the 'Little People' bring food and water for her. It was put on at the L'Orient Festival in what then was the largest marquee in Europe. Richard also wrote a saga, Trystan, based on Trystan and Iseult.*

Merv's contribution was, with his wife Alison, as a member of the dance group, Cam Kernewek: *Anne Jeffery was a sell-out with an audience in the region of 7000 people. Cam Kernewek formed in 1979 in order to take a Cornish Dance display to the Pan Celtic Festival in Ireland and then to L'Orient in Brittany. Strictly speaking we were not the first contemporary dance groups as the Old Cornwall Societies did quite a lot in the 20's...*

Dance troupes like Cam Kernewek are now regularly involved with a number of Cornish festivals. Steve Hall, a regular at Piper's and another of Brenda Wootton's accompanists, was instrumental in helping to revive the Golowan mid-summer festival in Penzance in the early 90's. Merv: *Steve got us to bring our (Cam Kernewek's) Pen Glas (horse-skull hobby horse) to the first festival to encourage Penzance to re-create their own – which they did and there are several versions now. In fact there is another connection with Brenda in that whenever the opportunity arose to work together she would tell a spooky story to introduce our 'oss...*

The Davidstow piper. The first set of Cornish bagpipes made by Clive Palmer were based on the dual-chanter pipes in this 16th Century carving.

Clive Palmer and Bob Devereux early 1978.
Photo by Lesley Billingham.

The various music festivals that emerged in the 70's also provided a way for established musicians to keep in touch with each other. By 1975 Michael Chapman had made several more TV appearances including four on The Old Grey Whistle Test. Michael: *I met Jill Johnson with Pete Berryman because they were on the same circuit. So we'd meet up at festivals. I remember the Cambridge Folk Festival. In '73 Steeleye did it, in '74 Fairport did it, then in '75 they said 'we're not having any folk rock, we're not having any drummers'. I turned up with a 10-piece Memphis soul band. The crowd loved it but the organisers didn't. I've never been invited back there, put it that way!*

Mike Chapman, Rick Kemp, Martin Carthy, Norma Waterson at Norwich 1973. Brenda Wootton
is standing behind them.

Musically, Michael had travelled a long way from his club roots by
becoming an exponent of full-blown folk-rock. By a strange twist of
fate, 1976 saw him return to Cornwall to record his sixth album at
Sawmills studio, in the house that had previously been the Val Baker's
home.

Despite the popularity of rock and folk-rock, traditional folk-singing
continued unaffected by fashions, and in 1975 Peter Kennedy returned
to Cornwall 20 years after making the film 'Oss Oss Wee Oss' to record
'Boscastle Bow-wow' featuring Charlie Jose, Freddy Jewel, Evan
Trick, and Loxton Pickard.

Support for the folk clubs themselves was slowly declining, however.
The audiences that had happily filled them in the 60's and early 70's
had grown up and moved on, and in the process some of the original
energy and enthusiasm had been dissipated.

231

The two most important clubs, Piper's and The Folk Cottage, survived to the end of the decade, but only just. Mic McCreadie: *I was resident singer at Piper's from around 1971, until it slowly dwindled away in the mid-eighties. I remember it being held in The Turk's Head in Chapel Street Penzance (it went through various venues after it left The Great Western Hotel) and Denis Clixby, who made lots of recordings, being in charge both financially and in a management capacity...*

Fish: *Piper's went from The Great Western, to the London Inn (bottom of Causeway Head), to The Gulval Meadery, to the Old Quay House, Hayle Causeway and then to the Trencrom Revellers Hut where it fizzled out. Niall and Cathy Timmins ran the club for a while before Denis took over. The Folk Cottage went to Rose, then to Goonhavern, to Perranporth, then to The Swan in Truro. It fizzled out there.*

Noel Murphy: *Brenda was a force of nature. But when Brenda's health started to fail and she was no longer involved, the folk scene down here collapsed.*

John Sleep: *When the Folk Cottage moved to Rose, it changed its character from that moment on. Many of the artists that we'd been booking were now expecting bigger fees - they had agents and so on and we simply couldn't afford it anymore. The audience that we'd attracted went off to college, and the artists themselves also went onto the college circuit where they could be paid good money.*

Michael Chapman on the Old Grey Whistle Test c1974. Ralph McTell also made more than one appearance on the programme.

232

Fish and Brenda reunited for a gig with Alex Atterson and Roger Butler at The Swan in Truro. Late 70's.

Many of those whose careers had relied on the folk clubs started to struggle, having not been able to convert their popularity into subst-antial record sales. Wizz Jones: *I've put my whole life into this, and then at the end of it I've got nothing! I'm still in the same financial state I was in in 1958! But I'm not complaining. I was there at the very beginning, I had all those opportunities – I just didn't make the right moves.* Record collector 2004

Some diversified into new careers. Brenda Wootton and John the Fish both went on to have their own radio shows on Radio Cornwall in the 80's. Sue: *Brenda took her radio show very seriously indeed. She was on once a week and she put in hours and hours and hours of work. But it was her way of thanking Cornwall for everything, and also involving the Cornish people. She got a really big following from that.*

Brenda and Ralph both also made frequent appearances on TV in the 80's, Ralph as a co-presenter on a children's programme, and later as a special guest in a sketch on the French and Saunders comedy show. Noel Murphy also appeared as an actor in a number of well-known TV series, whilst Brenda's frequent appearances tended to be on more local TV stations. Sue: *She had a couple of special programmes. One was called 'Cornwall: the Land I Love'. In it she interviews a couple of*

233

people in Newlyn about Allantide. Brenda remembered, as a girl, being given an Allan apple on Allantide: you would put under your pillow so you had sweet dreams.

Clive Palmer gave up professional music-making after C.O.B. broke up. He believes that, in terms of record sales, few folk musicians tasted true success: *Folk was never going to be a big deal. I remember when Steeleye Span were at the height of their career they were all broke. Folk was never going to be that big.*

Others suggest that by 1970 folk's commercial zenith had already passed. Mike Silver: *Acoustic music stopped being successful in terms of chart success towards the beginning of the 70's anyway. Dylan started the trend of writing protest songs, and a lot of people jumped on that bandwagon. But I just do what I do and I don't compromise. But I've never thought of what I do, and what my colleagues do as being aimed at a commercial market.*

Ralph McTell was the exception to prove the rule. His commercial success peaked at the end of 1974 when he had a number two hit in the UK with 'Streets of London'. The song, which had been re-recorded with orchestral accompaniment, reached number one in several other countries, and its success cemented Ralph's reputation.

Wizz: *Ralph did well. He deserved to. He actually lived my dream. I always used to say to Ralph that I really love Cornwall, I'd like to have a house in Cornwall and a flat in London and Ralph really did that. He lives my dream and I'm just stuck here in London!*

The hit version of the song, which was included on Ralph's seventh album 'Streets of London' had not come completely out of the blue. In 1972 he had changed record labels and in 1973 his brother, Bruce, had taken over from Jo Lustig as his manager. Then, earlier in 1974, he played at some larger-scale venues, including a 6500-seater sell-out concert at The Royal Albert Hall.

Ralph's timing was good, but he could not have left it much longer, because folk as a pop-genre was falling out of fashion. Following on from glam rock, punk was essentially an urban music heavily promoted by a London-based music-press. In contrast to folk, it did not have a natural home in Cornwall.

Fish: *There came a point when I counted up as many as 16 folk clubs in Cornwall - lots open 3 or 4 nights a week and the whole thing became very diffuse. Whether that was the cause of the demise I can't say, but it reflected the country-wide situation, where folk fell out of favour for some reason.*

However 'folk' as a genre, though not often called this any more, has made a comeback. In the last 10 or so years the acoustic guitar, and other more traditional folk instruments, have once again become the instruments of choice for many young musicians and song-writers. The local music scene is again strong, and Cornwall has played a role in the success of a number of high-profile performers, providing important early gigs for Newton Faulkner, and being home to both James Morrison and Ben Howard at formative stages in their careers.

A new generation have rediscovered COB, Wizz Jones, and Ralph McTell. Devendra Banhart has covered songs by Clive Palmer, and in 2011 Thurston Moore of Sonic Youth paid Michael Chapman the ultimate compliment by organising a tribute concert and album for him. This has triggered renewed interest in the US.

But the true legacy of the closely-knit Cornish folk-family of the 60's lies in the wealth of records and recordings that were made at the time. To paraphrase Whispering Mick Bennett as, in his memoirs, he recollects those special years in the caravans at Mitchell and chalets at Sawmills: *We were a part of the cultural upsurge of new voices in the 1960's and 70's and against all the odds (the recordings) seem to have stood the test of time.*

Those years now exist in my mind's eye as a journey remembered for the changes rang, when the ordinary rarely impinged upon our lives, and our senses were never dulled by any forced regime. The albums we made during those years, go some way to represent our achievement, but voyages of discovery often don't find the prize they set out to search for. I think our prize was the journey itself.

Appendix: The most significant records of the 60's and early 70's as associated with folk performers who lived in Cornwall or played in Cornwall as 'resident musicians' (roughly chronological order). All are described in the text, and most are now available as CD's.

Singing at the Counthouse EP *Compilation*
More singing at the Counthouse *Compilation*
*16 Tons of Bluegrass *Wizz Jones & Pete Stanley*
Piper's Folk *Compilation*
*Catch The Wind *Donovan*
*Mayflower Garland *Cyril Tawney*
*Banjoland *Clive Palmer (recorded in 1967, released in 2005)*
Wizz Jones *Wizz Jones*
*8 Frames a Second *Ralph McTell*
*Sunshine Possibilities *Famous Jug Band*
*The Legendary Me *Wizz Jones*
*Spiral Staircase *Ralph Mc Tell*
Chameleon *Famous Jug Band*
Sky in My Pie *John James and Pete Berryman*
Daylight *Daylight*
Pasties and Cream *Brenda Wootton & John the Fish*
*Rainmaker *Michael Chapman*
Mike Silver *Troubadour*
*Spirit of Love *COB*
*Sole Survivor *Michael Chapman*
*Moysche McStiff and the Tartan Lancers of The Sacred Heart *COB*
*My Side of Your window *Ralph McTell*
Crowdy Crawn *Brenda Wootton & Richard Gendall*
No Song to Sing *Crowdy Crawn*
*Lazy Farmer *Lazy Farmer*
Ceolacanth *John the Fish*
Starry Gazey Pie *Brenda Wootton & Robert Bartlett*

*available as CD re-releases.